PRAISE FOR *SUNLIGHT BURNING AT MIDNIGHT*

"In her moving memoir, Jessica Ronne reminds us that life circumstances, whatever they may be, are simply narratives of a much larger story. One which encompasses the ebb and flow of faith, grace, redemption, and restoration."

—DOUGLAS MANN,
ARTIST AND AUTHOR OF
THE ART OF HELPING OTHERS

"Jessica's heartbreaking yet inspiring story reminds me that if we hold on to God and his promises, he indeed redeems *everything* we dare to place in his hands. I highly recommend Jessica's book as it encourages us to believe for the best, no matter what the circumstances."

—NANCIE CARMICHAEL,
MULTI-PUBLISHED AUTHOR OF
*SURVIVING ONE BAD YEAR: SPIRITUAL
STRATEGIES TO LEAD YOU TO A
NEW BEGINNING*

"Some stories lead us to the opening of empty tombs and paint the unexpected sunrise of God's love in the darkness. Jessica Ronne's remarkable book, *Sunlight Burning at Midnight*, is just such a story. Readers will weep, laugh, and wonder at God's way of shaping a beautiful life out of death, disappointment, and despair in a young mother's life. Get this book for yourself, for anyone who suffers in God's presence, for anyone who has lost love, and anyone who needs a word of hope. The author's words invite us into her story: 'Ultimately, it is a story of the sun rising in the midst of the darkest of nights, the midnight hour at times, to display God's glorious plan and wisdom so beautifully. At the deepest levels this is a story of redemption; redemption from pain, loneliness, despair, and ultimately, redemption from control.'"

—MADOC THOMAS,
RETIRED MINISTER AND COUNSELOR;
AUTHOR OF *CLIMBING HOME:
FROM VALLEYS OF DESPAIR TO
MOUNTAINS OF HOPE*

"This book is a call to full consciousness, to stop slumbering through life and see the present moment as a gift. This book is about living with contentment in the face of unspeakable tragedy. But this book is, above all, about hope. Jess shows us that hope isn't a doctrine. It's a person, Jesus. And we don't need to demand a perfect life because we have a perfect Hope. Don't we all need that reminder? I know I do."

—FRANK POWELL,
FREELANCE WRITER; BLOGGER
AT WWW.FRANKPOWELL.ME

sunlight burning at midnight

a memoir

jessica ronne

Deep River Books
B O O K S

Published by
Deep River Books
Sisters, Oregon
www.deepriverbooks.com

ISBN: 9781940269986
Library of Congress: 2016952947

Printed in the USA

Cover design by Connie Gabbert

DEDICATION

To those who mourn:
Lift up thine eyes.

To my son, Lucas, "bringer of light":
May your story always shine brightest in the darkest moments.

To Ryan:
Till we're old and gray.
God willing.

To Him be the glory.

CONTENTS

INTRODUCTION

"I am the Lord who heals you."

Exodus 15:26

The day was beautiful—that summer morning in 2008, the sun streaming through the large bay window as Martha, my son Lucas's caseworker, and I reviewed his medical coverage for the upcoming year. We talked about Lucas, how he was doing with his therapies, and whether or not he had any specific needs for adaptive equipment. As our conversation progressed, the heartaches and struggles of two separate lives began to unfold.

Four years prior, Lucas had been terminally diagnosed before his life had even begun. I now had secondhand experience with numerous brain surgeries involving Lucas and my husband, along with the burden of near financial ruin as we struggled to keep our heads above water through many tough economic and personal hardships. The past four tumultuous years had brought worry, fear, mounting medical bills, and stress on our marriage and our lives.

As Martha's and my connection deepened, she shared her personal tragedies, including the death of her husband and her daughter's current battle with cancer.

In the midst of our conversation I quietly mentioned that I had kept a journal during my pregnancy with Lucas. Looking up, compassionate tears welling in her eyes, she said, "You need to have that published so people know there is hope. People always need to know miracles can occur and they can never, ever lose hope."

So here it is, Martha, finally, eight years after our meeting. This book grew to include not only those initial journal entries with Lucas but also reflections and thoughts that occurred later as I stood beside my husband Jason as he battled cancer. I begged the Almighty for a physical healing, and yet ultimately watched him succumb to a different kind of healing, just as Lucas had been healed far differently than my human comprehension could have ever grasped in those moments.

Perhaps you too carry burdens. Perhaps you need to know that you do not ever, ever have to lose hope, and you must not. Perhaps you grapple with answers and healings that are different from what you desired. This story is for you. A story that defies everything that seems to make sense according to a human perspective. A story that displays something as miraculous as sunlight burning at midnight.

Over time, my story has unfolded to include three distinctly different healings revealed one by one, all of which defy many of our traditional Christian theologies and thoughts surrounding what healing should look like. These healings are not the neatly packaged versions so often prayed for; instead they are gloriously messy versions seeping with redemption, achieved painfully with layer upon layer of faith and grace at the core.

My story represents hope in the raging storms of life, and hope after the storm subsides—the calm that brings a peaceful, gray ache. Ultimately, it is a story of the sun rising in the midst of the darkest of nights, at the midnight hour at times, to beautifully display God's glorious plan and wisdom.

The first part of this story, my beginnings, I tell you so you can understand where I come from and how I found myself on this journey. Later, I share journal entries from 2004, written as I carried unborn Lucas through the final four, lonely months where I felt every kick, punch, and glimmer of life and yet knew that the child I carried safely within my womb had already been pronounced dead by the experts. The proclamations of numerous specialists still ring in my heart: *"You should consider abortion. These babies have a way of*

*eliminating themselves. Try again. Vegetative state at best. "*Within this
first journey I battled with faith, hope, and God Almighty, ultimately
surrendering, although not very quickly or willingly, to his care for
my tiny unborn child.

The second part of the story includes my late husband's battle
with cancer and how I learned to rely on God's grace and mercy in
the midst of intense pain and questioning. This was a journey of three
tumultuous years of caring for four young children while striving to
maintain a shred of faith as my young husband succumbed to the
disease eating away at his body. The story is raw, drenched with real
feelings as I waged war once again with the Almighty, repeatedly asking *"Why?"* in the darkest hours of despair, weeping in brokenness at
what God had asked of me in this life.

Finally, the last part of the story is in the present: the beautiful,
redemptive today, with all that hindsight offers as I see how God wove
so much brokenness together: broken marriages, broken children,
families ripped apart, and extreme heartache. He wove the messiness
into something remarkably beautiful.

At the deepest levels, this is a story of redemption: redemption
from pain, loneliness, despair, and ultimately control. Wherever we
are in life, whatever unfamiliar road we travel against our wills, whatever painful news is spilled upon our ears unexpectedly, whatever difficult decision we have to make, it is not in our hands. Remember, he
is in control—always—and he will be faithful to see you through to
the other side, either in this life or the next.

CHAPTER 1

Ignorant Bliss

"The righteous will live by faith."

Romans 1:17

I walked into the ultrasound room and felt the complete absence of warmth. No beauty relieved the coldness, no picture of a mother holding a child or a sunset over the water. Nothing to remind those who nervously waited of the potential for joy within the world.

A large, heavyset woman poked with her stubby fingers at my thin, slightly rounded body. As the silence continued to descend, the air thickened with unspoken thoughts. I looked at this doctor, the expert I had been sent to, repeatedly trying to catch her eye, to shake her unmovable countenance. I wanted to see a glimpse of understanding in her cold stare, but she refused to make eye contact. She refused to make me an individual. She refused to feel anything for me. And I began to despise her.

The pokes with her finger turned to prodding with the ultrasound wand as she silently walked about the room with an air of intellectual superiority, contemplating the defective nature of what lay within me. I found myself suffocating beneath her smugness and the uncomfortable silence, thinking about her large belly looming over me. I focused on her obesity to avoid thinking about the imperfection held within my womb, about the diagnoses around the corner.

I lay on the metal table, completely still, as she spoke in hushed tones with the nurse. The gravity of the situation began to set in. Hot, confused tears started to flow uncontrollably.

1

The doctor glanced at me and asked, "Where's your husband? He should be here for this news."

I explained, blubbering through tears, that we hadn't realized the severity of the situation, and he had remained home with our other son.

The doctor stretched out her plump arm and began drawing repetitive circles on the whiteboard, a demonstration of how she viewed my baby's predicament. I sat there feeling like a child who was failing miserably at a particular subject in school, but the subject I was failing was that of being pregnant. My teacher drew a large head representing the accumulated fluid and then continued to draw circles around that head, signifying continued growth as the fluid increased month by month. I half-expected her to draw a big *BOOM* with scribbles and chaos as the head ultimately exploded.

She didn't. She simply said, "If I were you, I would take care of it and try again. You are a healthy young girl, and you won't have any problems getting pregnant. In fact, you will be doing this baby a favor, because these kinds of fetuses have a way of spontaneously aborting themselves. They are not supposed to make it. It's just nature's way."

* * *

My life began in 1977 in Grosse Point, Michigan, a small, wealthy suburb on the outskirts of Detroit. I was born to Jim and Tammy, two people joined together not only in love but also through the undeniable fact that they would soon be blessed with their first child, approximately eight months after they spoke their wedding vows.

My mother, father, and I lived in Grosse Point as Dad studied his way through law school. My parents rented a small, two-bedroom home a few months before I was born on the street that separated the ghettos of Detroit from the lavish, million-dollar homes that sketched the Grosse Point skyline only blocks away.

After I made my appearance, Mom accepted her role as a home-maker while working part-time at a local elementary school, allowing Dad the opportunity to focus on his education. There wasn't a lot of extra money after the bills were paid. Later, when I was a teenager and money was no longer in short supply, Mom told a story about how she and Dad would often fight about butter during those early days. The thing was, Dad grew up with margarine. Mom grew up with butter—only butter. Mom believed that margarine was poison, while Dad took into account their strict budget when grocery shopping, and margarine was significantly cheaper than butter. Mom eventually won; I grew up with butter.

Two years after my birth, I became an older sister as twin brothers Zach and Zeke made their arrival. A few weeks after the twins were born, we moved west to Grand Rapids, where Dad began a promising career with a local law firm.

Within the next few years, our family grew considerably with the additions of another brother, Elijah, and four more sisters: Hannah; a second set of twins, Chelsea and Chloe; and the baby, Greta. We lived in an old, renovated house in the city until Hannah was born and then moved to the other side of town, taking up residence in a 150-year-old farmhouse on ten acres, where we lived simply, cultivating a small hobby farm of sheep, dogs, cats, and chickens.

I went to the local public school until seventh grade, and then Mom and Dad decided to pursue homeschooling for the remainder of their children's education. I did not embrace this decision with optimism or joy. I appreciated the social aspect that school provided, but my siblings accepted the verdict with more enthusiasm, excited about the promises of "free time" and "sleeping in." My opinion might as well have been nonexistent. So began a dreary, lonely life of chores, schooling, and many solitary walks to reflect upon what I considered to be my pitiful plight.

Weekly highlights often included gardening, canning, or Saturday shopping with Mom and Grandma. Occasionally I opted to stay home during these outings, desiring instead to play with my brothers and sisters, and Dad would grant us free rein of the house as long as we left him alone to work in the study. Throughout the day, we experienced calm and relaxation as he solemnly concentrated on the next big deal he was constructing, and we, the lesser folk, did whatever we wanted to do without being harassed . . . until exactly thirty minutes before Mom was scheduled to arrive home. Then it all changed. From the office, an ominous figure would emerge in full force, frantically barking and hollering, "Clean up the mess, do the dishes, sweep the floor, pick up the snippets!"

(*Snippet,* n.: a small piece of something stuck in the carpet that would apparently bother Mom if she saw it.)

Dad didn't want to pay the price if Mom determined him negligent of child duty while she was out.

Since our family of ten traveled together on a daily basis, Dad and Mom invested in an extended eleven-passenger van. Mom insisted the white van was too ordinary and had a navy and purple stripe painted around the exterior. The color didn't bother me as much as the fact that we looked like a group departing from a mental institution whenever we went out together. It definitely did not help that my brothers found it hilarious to act like escapees from this institution, and while we drove down the road, they could be seen plastering their faces against the windows, tongues sticking out, arms flailing, and drooling incessantly in an attempt to make their oldest sister cringe in embarrassment and curse the life she was born into.

When I was sixteen years old, Mom and Dad began the process of adoption, and by the time I had reached my seventeenth birthday, Karen, fourteen years old, and Nathan, eleven years old, were introduced as our new siblings. The circus was formally adding to its brood. The next year, 1994, I officially graduated from homeschooling via ACT scores that determined a competent intelligence level. I began college the following year at Cornerstone University, a small Christian school in Grand Rapids, Michigan, choosing to live at home in order to save money.

Jason, who would become my future husband, and I met in May of 1999 when I started working as a front desk girl at a local athletic club. My friend, Mandy, had recently introduced me to strength training, and she suggested that I apply for a part-time job at the club where she worked—not so much for the minimum wage the position offered, but more as an opportunity to have a free membership along with the added bonus of meeting attractive guys. On my first day there, Mandy taught me how to check in customers, wash towels, operate the tanning bed, and cash out protein bars and smoothies. During a particularly quiet period, when the front door wasn't constantly ringing with people whisking in and out of the club, she leaned over and quietly whispered in my ear "Hey, there's that hot guy I was telling you about. He's headed this way."

The previous day, Mandy had informed me that there was this perfect guy at the club that she wanted to set me up with, and now he was headed straight towards us; exuding confidence in each bouncy step that he took, inching closer and closer. I glanced up and met his gaze as he sauntered near the desk. A hot flush came upon my cheeks, and I quickly ducked down to organize the already neatly folded towels. I realized I couldn't stay crouched like this forever, so within seconds, I slowly began my ascent back to noticeability.

"Hiya! Mandy!" he exclaimed loudly while jokingly slapping her backside with a sweaty towel. "Hey Jason!" she replied. I awkwardly stood beside her, not entirely sure where to rest my eyes as Jason and I both knew we were in the midst of a potential setup. I conducted a quick once-over. He was tall and attractive with jet black hair and deep blue eyes, and his body was slim and muscular from years of playing tennis and weight training. He kept smiling, glancing at me, and then smiling and glancing back at Mandy as if to say, *Okay, do what you're supposed to do, introduce me already.*

"Oh, yeah, Jason, this is my friend Jessica I was telling you about. Jess this is Jason."

I looked him square in eyes as I had been taught to do from childhood. "Nice to meet you," I said with a cocky grin. "I've heard quite a bit about you." I felt like I was looking at my future as we made our initial introductions and I thought, *I'm going to marry this boy someday.*

He returned my strong gaze with a gentle smile. "Nice to meet you, too. How's your first day on the job?"

"It's great so far," I replied, thinking, *It will be even better if you stick around for a bit.*

We continued small talk for a few minutes as Mandy excused herself to set up a customer for a tanning appointment. He was easy to talk with and full of charm. He told me about his full ride tennis scholarship at Western University, an accomplishment he was extremely proud of. He told me about his recent personal training certification. He told me about how his major was exercise science. He did almost all of the talking, which I was okay with as I slowly allowed the butterflies in my stomach to quiet their wings. I immediately noticed that he didn't have a confidence problem, and every word he spoke was uttered with clarity and pride until the end of our conversation. Only then did I notice a slight wavering of his confidence, a slight fumbling over his words, a hint of humility that accompanied the boyish grin on his lips.

"So, you think that maybe you want to come over for dinner Sunday and hang out at my family's pool?"

Our strong initial attraction grew rapidly as we discovered our common faith and enjoyment of many of the same activities such as working out, days at the beach, and fun nightclubs where he taught me to swing dance. One humid night in August of 1999, we had dinner at his family's house—which we did often, as were were both full-time students and only working part-time. His mom cooked a roast with mashed potatoes and corn, and after the meal, Jason asked if I wanted to go for a walk down to the gazebo at the end of their housing development. I agreed.

As we walked, he grabbed my hand. I couldn't believe how sweaty his palm was, and he kept muttering strange phrases as we strolled along.

"Is everything okay?" I asked.

"Yeah, I'm fine," he replied, but he didn't seem fine. My mind was racing: *What in the world? He's acting like a maniac.* Then it hit me. *Oh my word, he's going to propose!* I knew it, absolutely knew that was what was coming. We had discussed marriage a handful of times in our quickly-developing relationship, justifying our desire with the thought process of *When you know, you know* ... but, for the time being, I had to keep my cool, because we still had another ten minutes before we arrived at our destination. I started to get sweaty palms. *It's so soon, but I love him, what are our families going to think? Are we ready for this?* We stepped up onto the gazebo on that beautiful, dusk filled night, and he immediately dropped to one knee, beads of sweat pouring down his face and altering his otherwise very confidant and cool demeanor.

"Jess, I know we've only known each other a few months, but I love you. My parents love you, and I want to spend the rest of my life with you. Will you marry me?"

Of course I said yes. Neither of us were strong in the patience department, and both of us were type A firstborn children, which would serve us well as we made many life altering decisions together. We wasted no time. We were married that following April and officially began our lives together.

Jason and I were a perfect young married couple, and life was easy. Upon graduating from college the same year we were married, we decided to move to Detroit where he had a promising job opportunity working as a tennis professional and personal trainer while I struggled to determine what exactly I wanted to pursue. I had earned a degree in secondary education with a major in English and was offered numerous teaching positions, including one in the heart of the city. But I was young and naïve—and knew it—and the thought of working in this rough part of town was more than I could handle. I declined the position and many others as well. Honestly, I didn't want a full-time job. I wanted to continue dabbling as a writer, focus on being a wife, and soon, hopefully, contemplate the idea of motherhood.

We lived in Detroit for a short stint but soon realized we didn't feel settled miles away from friends and family. On a whim, a prayer, and a pinch of stupidity, Jason left a growing career, I left a potential tutoring opportunity, and we returned to Grand Rapids. I contacted a previous acquaintance and was quickly able to obtain employment as a receptionist with a local car dealership while he began working in insurance sales with his father. We found an apartment and settled into a nine-to-five daily existence, a different and difficult schedule after tasting a lifestyle of freedom in Detroit. The same year that we moved back to our hometown, Mom and Dad adopted two orphans from Haiti, Moses and Emma, making me legally the oldest of twelve children.

I discovered I was pregnant with our first child only months into our new life, but joy quickly turned to misery as the nausea and exhaustion began. I despised my job, which began at 6 a.m., five days a week, where I sat for eight hours and answered occasional phone calls from sophisticated gentlemen clientele. I tried to maintain an element of grace as they practiced their refined charm on an uninterested receptionist. Jason was no happier with his new career, which consisted of wearing a tie and dress pants while making cold calls to prospective clients all day. One day, we quit our jobs. Just like that. We had no backup plan and a baby on the way—it probably was not the wisest decision. We did have a little money saved, which allowed us to purchase a nice mobile home in a quaint trailer park in Jamestown, Michigan.

Jason quickly rebounded, landing another job as a personal trainer, and I obtained summer work babysitting for a local family. We were happy, making enough money, and finally becoming settled. I qualified for Medicaid, thereby eliminating any health insurance worries, and early that fall, before our first baby arrived, I was hired as an after-school director. We settled into life, living simply and idyllically in our modest three-bedroom trailer.

Our baby boy, Caleb, arrived in November of 2002 . . . though "arrive" is a very loose term. Two weeks late, he was finally forced out. I was scheduled for an induction the night of November 13, and like many first-time moms, I was determined to have a natural birth. The evening dragged on, and as I did not progress, I was administered Pitocin to encourage the process along. In my naïveté, I declined an epidural because "by golly, my mother had eight babies naturally, and I should be able to do this as well."

The Pitocin began increasing the contractions, and as they became harder and faster, I realized I probably should have agreed to something to help ease the pain. By this time I was completely doubled over in anguish. The torment of labor washed over my entire body, and the Pitocin wasn't allowing an ounce of mercy between contractions. I finally gasped, "Please tell the doctor I want an epidural!" To which the nurse replied, "Sorry, honey, you're too late. All you can do now is push."

I started to sob. I was in extreme pain, and as I pushed for the final fifteen minutes, I remember lying there on the hospital bed thinking, *This is what it feels like to die. I am dying. I have to be. This is not a pain humans were meant to endure. It has to be dying pain . . .* and with one final push, out came the most beautiful sight I had ever laid eyes on: my beautiful baby boy.

Caleb was an easygoing baby. Jason would bring him to work on nights when we were both busy, but for the most part I was able to stay home with him, enjoying our time together as I adjusted and blossomed into motherhood.

Jason had successfully negotiated ownership of a fitness club, his dream job, and we decided to reap the benefits of how well the business was doing by building a new home. We had made it. We considered ourselves successful in all aspects of life: careers, house, family, and marriage. We felt on top of the world. We were anxious to add to our family and ecstatic when we found out that I was pregnant again—just a little over a year after having Caleb.

We had no idea, then, how quickly life could change, or how messy redeeming it would become.

CHAPTER 2

The Journey Begins

*"He will love you, bless you, and increase your numbers. He
will bless the fruit of your womb, the crops of your land—
your grain, new wine and oil—the calves of your herd and
the lambs of your flocks in the land he swore to your forefa-
thers to give you."*

Deuteronomy 7:13

January 27, 2004

I have wonderful news! My second baby is on the way, and I
find out tomorrow when I'm due. I don't remember being this
tired with Caleb, but I probably was. I'm just whipped. Between
building a house, a one-year-old, and buying an investment
property, I'm not sleeping great. In a month we go to Florida,
and I can't wait! It's been three years since our last vacation. The
business is doing well, and I can't believe how blessed we are as a
family. It's amazing to me. Caleb is growing stronger every day,
but he won't say mama yet. Oh well . . .

February 13, 2004

I'm about eleven weeks tomorrow and due Sept 27. I'm finally
sleeping a little so I feel better. We received our preapproval letter for the house. That was a big step, and now we're trying to
pull our deposit together before we start building. We picked

out a huge dining room table for our "big" family and the coolest front oak door.

Life was busy, and I didn't feel well. I am not an enjoyable pregnant woman, and those around me are aware of all my discomforts. I have extreme morning sickness, I don't sleep well for nine months because of raging hormones, and I contract numerous skin diseases: ringworm, severe eczema, and random rashes. Finally, I do not enjoy monitoring every single activity my body does or does not do because of someone growing inside of me.

At the same time I felt the pressure to be mentally and physically capable for everything involved with the house construction, Jason's business, moving into a temporary apartment, and raising an active two-year-old. I resigned from my job as after-school director which added a few more needed hours to my days. I spent my newly free mornings packing, picking out materials for the house, or calling contractors. Once the afternoon arrived, I was sprawled out on the sofa watching mindless television, attempting to get a little rest from our hectic life.

One day, bored and devoid of energy, I decided to continue the tradition I had begun with Caleb and started to crochet my unborn baby a blanket. We had embraced leaving the gender unknown in both pregnancies, making Caleb's blanket a neutral white and this baby's a mint green. The decision to crochet the blanket turned out to be a blessing in disguise, providing me with a huge distraction. Even today this blanket is a beloved object.

April 2, 2004

Thirteen days until my twenty-seventh birthday. I can't believe it! The remainder of my twenties I will be busy making a family (we're thinking four babies), and in my thirties I can relax and get back to myself. My sister and I bought our first rental property. Hopefully I can prove to Jason that it's worth it. We get our final blueprints back in a week, and then we break ground on the house. We're moving into an apartment on April 26, and I can't wait to be moved so I can focus on Caleb, the baby, and the house. I started to feel the baby move and it's very exciting. It makes the whole experience so much more believable.

I could get through the morning sickness, I knew. Life lay ahead of us: four babies and relaxation as I entered my thirties.

Everything was going according to plan—until May.

May 8, 2004

I am devastated. We found out yesterday that our baby has hydrocephalus, a term completely unknown to me previously. It is water on the brain—too much water in the ventricles—and a small cerebellum, which breaks down into almost certain brain damage and death. I'm heartbroken but hopeful. Now we have four months, and our motto has become, "When God heals this baby." We are believing and praying for a miracle and believing that "God's not finished knitting this baby together yet." We are claiming verse after verse: "All things are possible to him who believes," and "Ask and these things shall be given to you"; "By his stripes we are healed."

I'm truly learning what it means to pray without ceasing. We are claiming victory over Satan, and we believe that we will have a testimony to shout to the world. That being said, I'm going for a second opinion on May 14. The doctors will be amazed at the progress of this baby. The baby kicks me often, signaling strength and determination, and that gives me strength. We have a huge army of prayer partners, and by faith we will overcome this.

I don't know if I was in denial of how bad the initial prognosis was, but for whatever reason, when I went for a second opinion, I went alone. I drove to the appointment with butterflies swirling in my stomach, which I tried to dismiss as "just nerves." I tried to pray, but my mind wandered. I hurriedly walked through the massive parking garage, trying to find stairs or an elevator to take me to my destination. I located the elevator bank, and as I stepped within its close confines, I felt like I was stepping into a coffin.

I found the clinic and opened the door, the faces glancing up at me from their reading materials, all looked concerned or dismal. I thought, *Why do these women all look so sad? Do they all have problems with their babies?*

Soon I heard my name being called. *Jessica Crisman!* I mindlessly went through the height and weight checks until the nurse led me to the cold ultrasound room, no beauty, no warmth— where I was met with that large, heavyset doctor, poking and prodding me with her stubby fingers.

I lay numb on the cold table—still, hot, confused tears flowing as I began to understand that the situation was dire. She asked where my husband was, and I replied that he had stayed home with our two-year-old son, and then she began drawing those repetitive circles, over and over and over again.

Drew circles and told me I should abort and try again.

As if her words had tapped into some reservoir of strength, I dusted myself off emotionally and methodically managed to transfer my body off the cold table. I wiped away any remaining tears, and in true Jessica style stuffed my pain into the deepest corner of my soul.

"Thank you," I quietly and politely whispered as I took hold of the checkout papers she handed me. I went through the motions, handed the receptionist the papers, made another appointment, and acted like I was in no way special or to be pitied. I was just one of the normal, everyday pregnant mothers, here with her normal unborn baby. I didn't allow myself to have a single thought about what I had just heard, denying all of it in that moment, and proceeded straight toward the elevator.

Alone inside its chambers, I stood quietly braced against the wall. *How in the world did this happen? How do two young, healthy people make a dead baby?* Struggling to hold back tears once again, I realized I couldn't remember where I had parked the car. I looked around, aimless, completely lost—lost in the parking garage, lost in life, and feeling like I was losing my mind. Finally locating the car, I managed to stumble toward the shelter that my maroon Dodge sedan would provide.

I slumped into the driver's seat with a deep sigh. Face tense from straining to keep the tears from exiting my eyes—straining to stay in control. I sat there for a moment and realized I had to let Jason know.

I pulled the car out, found the nearest gas station, and maneuvered as close to the pay phone as I could manage. Jason picked up and listened quietly as I choked out what the doctor had said. "Are you okay to drive?" he asked. "I'll start praying."

Somehow I arrived home. I have no idea what I thought or did or prayed during that long thirty-minute drive, but I do remember walking inside our dingy, dark apartment, lined top to bottom with dark brown paint and dirty brown carpet, to find my husband on his knees beside our bed, praying. Praying for safety as I drove home, praying for our unborn baby, and praying for grace and strength to walk the road before us.

CHAPTER 3

Fork in the Road

"He who dwells in the shelter of the Most High will rest in the shadow of the Almighty."

Psalm 91:1

May 17, 2004

I have made a pact with this baby; I won't give up until he or she does. God wants us to love him for him, not for the things that he gives us. There is a reason for all of this, and I may not understand it until I get to heaven. The faith of a mustard seed can move the mountain; we just need a little water moved out of our baby's head. May 8—57 ml water, cerebellum measuring sixteen weeks; May 14—42 ml water, cerebellum measuring twenty-two weeks. My friend Mindy was given the same diagnosis at four months' pregnant. The doctors predicted severe mental retardation or death, and her daughter is now eight years old and her only handicap is that she walks with crutches. Another friend was told the same thing and now has a perfectly healthy one-year-old daughter. As long as this baby's kickin', we're kickin'. I am telling everyone, "Keep me distracted." If I trust God to watch out for Caleb every day, I can trust him to watch out for this baby as well. It's going to be Abraham or David—Abraham with his son living, his faith having been tested, or David on his knees before God begging for his son's life until the moment God took his boy.

The next days and weeks were a blur. I made phone calls, sent out emails, and researched potential cures for my unborn baby. People didn't know what to say to me or how to respond. What do you say to a mom who is carrying a live baby but has been informed that the same baby will soon be dead? Do you congratulate her on the pregnancy? Offer condolences because the baby will probably die? A confusing situation that was even more confusing for me, the mom in question. Do I plan as if I will have a baby and absolutely refuse to accept the prognosis as truth, regardless of what the experts say, or do I begin to prepare my heart for my child's death?

The fork in the road lay before me, and I decided to take the harder route of believing that my child would live. Beyond a shadow of a doubt, he or she would live.

Psalm 91 became a daily source of encouragement. When I was worried, I would speak God's promises to myself: "I will not fear the terror by night or the pestilence or the plague, because the Lord is my refuge, and he promised that he would rescue me."

I read Scripture or listened to music, anything to wrap my mind around the truth of God's Word, declaring protection and safety for those who love the Lord and follow after him wholeheartedly.

May 19, 2004

I joined a message board today online about babies born with hydrocephalus, and it's been very helpful with information. It sounds like the water is decreasing according to the mothers out there who have gone through similar circumstances. Praise God!

Lessons I've been learning from the gospel of Luke: Luke 4—Lay hands on the sick, rebuke the condition. Jesus is willing, begging is allowed, faith of many people is helpful—action is directly related to faith. Luke 7—Plead earnestly with Jesus. Christ's heart goes out to the hurting. Luke 8—More pleading, "Don't be afraid, just believe and she will be healed." Luke 9—Begging, Luke 11:9–10, "Ask and it will be given to you, seek and you will find, knock and the door will be opened to you. For everyone who asks receives, he who seeks finds, and to him who knocks the door will be opened." Luke 17:6—Faith is a total dependence on God and a willingness to do his will. It is a complete and humble obedience to his will and a readiness to do whatever he calls us to do.

I would be in a fantastic place of faith and trusting on some days, in a place of avoidance on other days, and on occasional days needing constant reassurance. Jason grew weary of the talking in circles that I would often engage him in as a way to refresh my faith. Other women didn't, and he encouraged me to find some women with similar circumstances. One such woman, Tiffany, became a dear connection through another friend of mine. She had faced a similar diagnosis in her pregnancy with her daughter.

On one particular morning, I needed to be reassured that my situation could turn out okay. I put Caleb down for his morning nap, pulled up a chair on our deck, and called Tiffany. She had previously admonished me to *call anytime*, morning, noon, or night, and she would be happy to hold my hand through the journey.

Our conversations usually revolved around me begging for reassurance that my baby would be okay, and she would share her story, which included how she had pleaded with God to heal her baby mentally but told him she was willing to accept any physical ailments. God had answered her prayer. Her baby was born with a completely normal mental capacity but never learned to walk and was instead confined to a wheelchair her entire life.

That wasn't the full healing I hoped for, but I enjoyed the reassurance that a diagnosis of severe hydrocephalus was not necessarily a death sentence or even necessarily a sentence of any handicap. Things could turn out okay.

During those difficult, faith-building days, I was not present for my family. I set them aside: their needs, desires, and cries for a wife and mom. When I wasn't praying, I spent most of my free time reading the Bible and books on healing. I went through the motions as wife and mom, getting Caleb dressed, making meals, going grocery shopping, and cleaning the apartment. But when my husband and son spoke, I prayed; when they laughed, I rebuked Satan with God's promises; and when they reached for me, I reached for my Bible. I withheld myself and justified it because I needed to give God exactly what he required in return for healing.

That was all that mattered to me.

CHAPTER 4

Downtrodden Faith

"Don't be afraid; just believe."

Mark 5:36

May 21, 2004

The whole thing completely sucks today. I hate everything about this situation. I hate waiting; I hate wrestling with all of the scenarios, with my faith, with my ability to have patience and to trust God. I hate trusting God today. I want it over. Then a little voice reminds me that if it's over, then there's no longer hope for a miracle. This is the worst part of my life ever. I hate it!

Today I can't handle a severely mentally challenged child, and I'm begging God to please not give me that. We need a miracle on Tuesday when we go to the third specialist. The water has to go down, or I think I'll go crazy. I swear this is a test, and I'm failing. Why can't I be a normal woman with a normal pregnancy and normal children? Why me? Why now in the middle of things going so well in our lives?

It's so easy to trust God in the good times, so I guess the real times of testing come in situations like this, but this time is just dragging . . . just make it to June. I'm learning that Jesus had pity on people (Luke 17) and that we must thank him in all situations. Luke 18:7–8—"Will not God bring about justice for his chosen ones who cry out to him day and night? Will he keep putting them off? I tell you, he will see that they get justice and quickly."

May 23, 2004

Baby shower for Aunt Susan, and everyone is supportive and sad about the news. My prayer today is that this baby experiences abundant life, wherever that may be, either here on earth or in heaven. DREADING Tuesday, another specialist, barely hoping for miraculous news but preparing to hear the worst again. I hope that's not unbelief, but I'm just trying to be practical and realistic. My prayer tonight: "Lord, grant me peace and may your favor shine upon my family, be gracious to us and bless us with a miracle."

The baby shower was an obligation I couldn't avoid, and the occasion was miserably awkward. My aunt, in her forties, was pregnant with her first child, while I, the young, healthy one, was carrying the child with a death sentence. It was like a cruel joke. It seemed as if everyone was uncomfortable with my presence. They would lovingly look upon me with pity-filled eyes, searching for the right words of comfort to offer. The situation was incredibly painful for me, the woman with the dead child in her uterus at a baby shower.

I came home knowing more clearly than ever that the battle wasn't over. I was determined to have my child just as she was going to have hers. I quoted Ephesians 6:10–11 to myself: "Finally, be strong in the Lord and in his mighty power. Put on the full armor of God, so that you can take your stand against the devil's schemes." Another visit to the specialist was just around the corner.

May 26, 2004

I never went to the specialist, because they don't take my insurance, so the next appointment is June 15. We're praying for a miracle! We broke ground yesterday at our house and that's a nice distraction. Baby is still kicking and moving a lot! I'm learning to cast my cares on God, not to worry, to be faithful, whatever the outcome, for when I see Jesus I want to hear, "Well done good and faithful servant." I want to run my race on earth and finish with a crown of glory. God's response to Job has been helpful, we won't and can't understand God's ways, but it doesn't matter, they are his ways. This is his child, and I am blessed to carry a precious gift. I told Jason I feel like Frodo in the movie *Lord of the Rings* with the responsibility of carrying the ring. I don't know why I've been chosen for this task, but I have been, and I will be faithful to the task until it is complete. The mother side of me desperately wants to bring a healthy baby home in three months, but the child of God in me demands faithfulness and trust in whatever outcome God has determined for our lives. We feel the multitudes praying because we are usually surrounded with peace. Jesus said, "Do not be afraid, just believe." Trials mold the human spirit, they make us authentic people.

May 29, 2004

Three days have passed! We feel the prayers of so many people, and we are so at peace. We have learned to let each day hold only the worries and problems of the day. If Jesus takes this baby home, I've made peace with my Savior being his or her father. I will see my baby again, but I'm still trying to have hope for a miracle. I believe that Christ's will be done. I feel more human through this time of suffering, and I'm trusting Jesus to turn my mourning into dancing.

May 30, 2004

My heart is really aching for my baby tonight. I feel like this situation is doing horrible things to Jason. He's short-tempered, and he's using words he doesn't normally use. I don't know, maybe I'm just sensitive. I want this baby desperately tonight. I want to go home from the hospital with a baby. At dinner we saw an older girl in a wheelchair acting like a two-year-old and drooling with a sippy cup. I don't think I can handle that, yet I want to be faithful to whatever God has for me. It's a struggle right now. I want a complete miracle. I want the miracle to be God's will. I think of all the good a miracle could do versus the death of this baby. I don't even like to think about being pregnant right now. It's not a happy time, and while I can usually take it one day at a time, today is hard. I don't know how anyone facing the death of their child wouldn't come into the throne room of the heavenly Father and beg for mercy.

The battle was unrelenting. Every day, every moment, I felt the weight of it. I grew desperate—not just for a victory, but for reprieve in the midst of the battle. Thankfully, God was willing to give it.

CHAPTER 5

Rain

"You heavens above, rain down righteousness;
let the clouds shower it down.
Let the earth open wide,
let salvation spring up,
let righteousness grow with it;
I, the Lord, have created it."

Isaiah 45:8

June 1, 2004

Made it to June . . .

I've asked myself today, is this a good moment in life? I keep remembering parts of life and how they were good because I hadn't heard about the baby yet. I have to say, life is bittersweet right now. There are extremely good aspects: Caleb, Jason, his business, our house—all roses in this life overshadowed by a dark cloud with the baby issues, but then I remind myself that dark clouds bring rain and rain brings growth and greater beauty through the blooming of the roses. If we're faithful through this I believe we'll feel the rain, we'll grow, and we'll bloom even brighter and more beautiful than before.

Later that day . . .

This has to be the worst pregnancy experience, feeling life yet being told that the same life I feel is surely going to die. I feel life in Caleb every day, but surely he must someday die just as this baby will die someday. His sentence is the same as all of ours. In living we must all die unless Christ returns. Today I cried painfully again, praying please heal this baby or please take the baby to heaven if healing is not in your plan.

That particular afternoon I fingered some of the baby's clothes, forgotten and tucked away within a drawer, feeling the softness and the innocence that the smooth fabric represented, and I just lost it. Caleb was in the other room watching a movie, Jason was at work, and there I was, in a heap on the brown, dirty floor, big, pregnant, and sobbing.

A random thought occurred: *I could kill this baby with convulsing if I don't stop.* I literally believed I could cause a miscarriage if I didn't stop wailing.

Everything within me was fighting for this child's life, so it seemed counterproductive to do anything that might jeopardize what I was ultimately fighting for. I wiped away the wetness on my face with dry hands, stood to my feet, and pushed the pain to the deepest crevices of my soul while carrying on throughout the day.

Life, I thought, was a storm. I had to walk through it somehow.

June 6, 2004

"Expect the rain"—a word at church last night, thank you Jesus! Saturday before the church service I believe I was under an intense attack from the enemy. I was so sick but went to church anyway. I learned so much on healing. It is God's will, claim it, be persistent, be strong, believe in your spirit and then walk away and say it over and over. Rebuke the devil in Jesus's name. A woman prayed over me and asked, "Are you having a boy?" I replied that I wasn't sure, and she answered, "I just saw a little boy playing baseball." We believe and stand firm for healing for this baby. Baby's kicking and moving a lot!

I was so sick over the weekend—typical flu symptoms in full force with an achy body, chills, fever, and a sore throat. I had heard about the healing service weeks earlier and was convinced that my baby would be healed at this gathering and that I needed to attend. When I became ill, I knew it had to be the devil trying to keep me from getting to the service. I went regardless of how I felt. It was undoubtedly inconsiderate to expose those around me to my symptoms, but I couldn't take the chance that my baby would miss a miracle.

I sat on the front row with Jason, Caleb, and my mother-in-law, Holly. Holly held Caleb while I tried to get as comfortable as possible on the hard wooden pew. I looked around the large, modern auditorium, decorated with peaceful, sky-blue paneling—a room the church budget committee had obviously spared no expense with. I avoided eye contact with those around me, feeling as if eye contact could elicit an unwanted conversation about my pregnancy.

I wiped wet hands on my skirt, trying to swallow away a dry mouth, anxious about all of the faces around me and over the possibility that absolutely nothing would happen tonight and I would leave the service brokenhearted and discouraged. I was also excited over the possibility that something could happen and a miracle of healing might occur for my baby.

My nerves escalated, and I began to shake, an uncontrollable convulsing, my head wobbling like my unborn child's would later do. I shook and sobbed, black mascara dripping down my wet face as I sat in the front row at that megachurch.

As a conservative, introspective control freak, this was not an enjoyable experience. It was, however, an enlightening one. In that crazy moment, God's Spirit quietly reassured me, *You have no control. Let it go and let me be Sovereign Lord, and I will show myself mightily to you.*

The minister called forward those who desired prayer, and I stumbled down the aisle—big, pregnant, sobbing, shaking me. I must have looked severely challenged, mentally and physically, but for once I didn't care. I didn't care how I looked to my husband, or to my mother-in-law, or to the whole congregation. I needed anything and everything that the Spirit was going to do through any person in that room, and I was going down to receive it for my child.

That's when the word came: *expect the rain.*

I was anointed and prayed over by various people and elders, but one woman in particular stood out in my mind. This woman gently laid her hand on my large belly, looked me directly in the eyes and asked, "Are you having a boy?"

"We don't know," I replied.

She paused, a look of steel confidence flashing in her eyes. "God just showed me a picture of a little boy playing baseball, and I believe I saw your son."

Throughout the remainder of my pregnancy, I desperately clung to that image of a beautiful, little boy playing ball.

June 8, 2004

I went to Walmart and a cashier said, "Oh are you having a boy?" I replied that I wasn't sure. A minute later as I was walking out of the store a mother was yelling at her little boy, "Lucas, Lucas, come here!" Thank you God for little signs of hope, for we had recently decided on the name Lucas if the baby were a boy.

June 9, 2004

Lucas means "Bearer of Light." He could be our miracle baby who brings the light of Jesus to many. That's our prayer.

During these days I was often praised for my superhuman strength, but really, that strength was built with layers of pain and growth. Every day I would awake from sleeping, run to the Word of God, and devour whatever I read. Through those words and my tears, I would desperately seek to trust that God would remain faithful and that life would continue moving forward in a cycle of joy and pain. Over time, that belief brought a strength that was continuously refined as gold.

CHAPTER 6

In the Thick of the Fight

"Be joyful in hope, patient in affliction, and faithful in prayer"

Romans 12:12

June 11, 2004

Our specific prayer for Tuesday's appointment is this—We are going to leave with joy in our hearts and a testimony. We are believing that the water is gone and the pregnancy is normal. "A season of suffering is a small price to pay for a clear view of God." Max Lucado

June 12, 2004

To do the will of God right now is to be faithful and to trust in him completely. I feel at peace. I hope it's not the calm before the storm. I feel peaceful in my days, in my moments, and in my nights. I pray steadily for the baby, but in a peaceful way, not the gut-wrenching prayers anymore. I pray desperately that this baby is healed on Tuesday (at the doctor's appointment), but I also believe desperately in God's timing, purpose, and will for our lives. I trust in that fact and that he will still be Lord of all, tomorrow, next year, and ages from today. The baby moves within me, and that means we continue to have a spiritual battle to fight. We will wage war as long as this baby's heart is beating.

As I finished writing those words, I put the journal away, turned off the music, and gazed out the window. I sat in the stillness, my two-year-old napping in the adjoining room.

I didn't understand the peace I felt. It had been such a journey to get here, but I was sure, in this moment, that my child was healed. Sure he had been healed from the day God created him and placed him in my womb. The faith in my heart to declare that I would have a live baby—it had to be from God!

That realization set me free: no longer did I need to twist the arm of Almighty God to serve my limited ideas. Even if my baby was severely challenged, God would strengthen me to mother him.

June 14, 2004

I put Caleb down for a nap, and now I'm preparing to pray and read the Bible. Our appointment is at 11:45 tomorrow. I'm hopeful that the water will be gone or decreased, and I'm scared of my reaction if it's not. I get teary-eyed thinking about it. I wish that God could be reasoned with, because I don't think that I have the energy to wait until the midnight hour for healing, but I'll take it if it comes that way. This is the saddest, most hopeful, and truly the most glorious hour of my life. I want a baby to go home with more than anything, well almost anything. I've come to a point in my walk with Christ through all of this where I want to be faithful to him more than anything. I do believe in his power to heal our baby. I don't understand why he wouldn't heal him or her, because from my worldly perspective more good would come from a healing than a death. My faith cannot rest on my wisdom but on the power of God.

June 16, 2004

Our appointment was yesterday, and the water has gone up. I put God in a box when I demanded a miracle in my time. I was angry, but I've decided to remain strong in faith and to keep praying the same prayer. I believe in Jesus's name that the water is removed and in Jesus's name the brain damage is extinct! The doctor started talking about options, so it looks like I'll be induced by August 12. That's a relief to hear. I'm not going to ask for ventricle numbers anymore, because I don't care. My faith will lie in the power of God and not in the wisdom of man, and I will declare that what was available thousands of years ago is still available today for this baby. I'm reaching out in faith and grabbing a hold of it!

Days before the appointment I prayed, every moment I was awake and with every toss of my weary body at night, saying, "In Jesus's name, the ventricles will decrease; in Jesus's name, the ventricles will decrease; in Jesus's name the ventricles will decrease."

The big day arrived when I believed I was going to see the manifestation of my faith. I laid my large, uncomfortable body in the slippery vinyl chair and heard the doctor's soft voice speak numbers indicating that the ventricles were increasing with fluid, and I thought, *No, that can't be right. I spoke it and believed it. Completely. I think . . . Is there something wrong with my faith? Do I not believe enough? Is God showing off? Making the baby worse so that the miracle can be bigger?*

I had so many questions. I believed that if I spoke it and believed it, then the baby would be healed. I was dumbfounded and angry. I went home and avoided God. I walked around our apartment numb, going about my normal daily duties of taking care of Caleb, going for a walk, cooking, and cleaning, but I certainly wasn't going to open my Bible or pray. If God was going to ignore my prayers, after everything I had done—all the faith I had mustered up!—then I wasn't going to acknowledge him.

This philosophy and anger lasted for a day. I woke up the next morning with my spirit refreshed, ready to begin the battle once again.

June 17, 2004

I've really entered into a battle. I see the enemy clawing for my baby, and I demand that he take his hands off. This is a child of God's and he is the baby's Creator, and by the blood of Jesus who defeated death and the grave, this baby will live! By his stripes this baby has life!

I'm trying to learn the meaning of faith, "being sure of what we hope for and certain of what we cannot see" Hebrews 11:1. I'm sure that this baby is alive now, and that is my hope for the future. I'm certain that I can't see the spiritual warfare surrounding this child, but I do feel it. Faith is a gift from God (Ephesians 2), and it is something to pray for (Mark 9).

My prayer is this, in the name of Jesus and by the power of Christ's blood, any spirit of brain damage and hydrocephalus, I command to be gone and never enter again. You have no place in our home, in our lives, or in this child's life. Jesus is the Creator, Healer, Savior, and Redeemer of this baby, and he says that he is the Lord our Healer, and by his stripes we are healed!

Jesus, give me faith to trust what I cannot see and make me certain of what is invisible. My faith declares that by the same power that raised Christ from the dead, this miracle is for me and for this baby. Heal this baby I pray, drain the water, and remove the brain damage in Jesus's name. Thy will be done on earth as it is in heaven.

CHAPTER 7

Faithfulness

"Cast all of your anxiety on him for he cares for you."

1 Peter 5:7

June 19, 2004

"My God, my God why hast thou forsaken me?" Matt 27:46. The moment Jesus took all death, disease, hydrocephalus, and brain damage upon himself. He went into hell and defeated Satan—the power IS in his blood. Jesus isn't a liar. He says, by his stripes we are healed. He is the Lord our Healer, don't be afraid, just believe. It's the power of the Holy Spirit working in me and in Jason and all the prayers. It's faith that comes through constantly depositing the Word of God into our spirits and then proclaiming, believing, and receiving that Word for this family.

June 22, 2004

I went to a healing class this morning that really pushed me out of my comfort zone. It was taught by a doctor who kept saying that he could see how strong my faith is. When he prayed for the baby, he prayed for hydrocephalus, brain damage, specifically that the water and head size decrease, and I never told him any of the diagnosis. All I said was that I was there for the baby. I choose to believe that my baby is healed, whatever that healing may look like in the end. I praise Jesus for that. I will keep praying for complete mental and physical restoration for this baby, and I will keep glorifying Jesus for the healing.

When I arrived home, there was a message from the doctor's office saying that they want to set up an MRI appointment for next Tuesday (healing class day). First I said no way. Too expensive—I want to go to class—I trust God and not an MRI. Then I started thinking—They called about twenty minutes after we were praying that this healing be manifested. Is God setting up an appointment to manifest it to me? So I said to God, if it is your will for me to skip class next Tuesday and go to the MRI, I need a clear sign by the doctor's office being absolutely adamant about me going. If it's not in your will, then they will call back and say it's not necessary. God is so good and he loves us so much. The enemy comes to steal, destroy, and kill.

I hesitantly walked into that first healing class. The class was held in a small gray room with one window facing the parking lot, the only view other than light, gray walls. The chairs were set up to face the podium in the front, about twenty blue and gray folding chairs, perfectly color-coordinated with the theme of the room. Outside of the podium and the chairs, the room could have easily passed for a clinical waiting room, with its bright fluorescent lights and appropriately-placed pictures of generic landscaping scenes.

I took my seat in the back row, avoiding eye contact with everyone just as most of the other people in the class were doing, each of us dealing with our own private pain and desperation—obviously the reason we were all gathered in this dismal room to begin with.

Up front, the man I presumed was the teacher was practically bouncing with anticipation as we waited for the final people to trickle in and take their seats. The bouncing man was a doctor—in his forties, saved from a youthful life of hell-bound activities, sex, drugs, and rock and roll. Once saved, he became a walking, talking, "Hallelujah, praise the Lord!" kind of testimony. His energy was inspiring and contagious and exactly what I needed.

The class was full of a variety of individuals: some who needed spiritual healing from addictions, some with mental problems, a few standing in proxy for others who needed healing, one woman who needed healing from the cancer cells ravaging her body, and other individuals who, it seemed to me, needed healing for ailments they could have readily fixed on their own with a little willpower. I struggled with their presence in the class.

A heavyset man named Walter, who was probably in his sixties, possessed a gentle old soul and extended a sense of calm and belonging to me. Week after week he would offer to pray with me and bring small inspirational books and notes as gifts, one inscribed with words from Exodus, "Then Moses said, "I pray thee, show me thy glory!" He knew from what I had shared with the class that I wanted God's glory to shine to the ends of the earth with my baby's ultimate healing.

Yet for all of his kindness, Walter was one of those whose presence in the class posed a conflict for me. He needed healing for type 2 diabetes, almost assuredly brought on by his obesity. As we prayed for his healing, I felt sad and awkward for him. Everyone in the room seemed aware that he had brought the disease upon himself, and the good doctor even preached an entire message on health and wellness one day, teaching that proper nutrition could offset certain diseases— such as type 2 diabetes.

Being married to a health fanatic and personal trainer, I knew Jason would not have handled the conflict of this man's prayer request without speaking his mind. I was certainly aware of the slight absurdity of praying for divine intervention for something you could readily fix with diet and exercise.

In my prideful arrogance, I thought Walter should perhaps be praying for help to overcome the sin of gluttony. I was almost jealous of this man, thinking, *If I could fix my problem, I wouldn't be here. Life would be so much easier if I could simply take matters into my own hands and fix this baby rather than having to completely rely on God for miraculous healing.*

A few months after the class, I read that Walter had been healed from his condition—he had passed away over the weekend from diabetic complications.

His death sobered me and made me realize how much Walter had relied on God in his weakness. He'd had it right. I wondered if I did.

June 24, 2004

I am so at peace and full of joy. The baby is moving, and no MRI is necessary. Jesus is the Creator and Healer of this baby, and I praise him. I set up the baby crib today as an act of faith. I also took Caleb's old baby clothes out of bins and placed them in drawers. I've been in such an intense battle and growing state for the past two months that I really know that now I have to be still and know that God is God. God is God yesterday, today, and tomorrow, and he doesn't lie. [We have] "a faith and a knowledge resting on the hope of eternal life, which God, who does not lie, promised before the beginning of time" Titus 1:1–2. So if God doesn't lie, then, "Whoever says to this mountain, be removed and cast into the sea and does not doubt in his heart but believes that those things he says will be done, he will have whatever he says. Therefore, I tell you, whatever you ask for in prayer, believe that you will receive it and it will be yours." Mark 11:23–24.

What a promise from God! How can that not be the most amazing thing to a Christian?

With no clear victory yet in sight, the journey had changed me, and maybe that was part of the grand plan all along.

God had to break me in order to mold me. This was a trial, a circumstance in life, and I'm thankful to have gone through it. It changed me from a lukewarm Christian to a Christian who yearns to be faithful. I continue to keep my eyes on Jesus, the author and finisher of my faith, and he guides my steps. Nothing else matters.

CHAPTER 8

Perseverance

"And let us not grow weary of doing good for in the proper time we will reap a harvest if we do not give up."

Galatians 6:9

July 3, 2004

Author Smith Wigglesworth says, "He who has brought you to this point will take you to the end." I am asking God for all things and believing that the water is gone. I'm claiming by faith, "If you believe you will receive whatever you ask for in prayer" Matthew 21:22. I do believe in God's Word, I believe that God keeps his Word, and so I believe the water is gone in the name of Jesus. God does not lie. Just as salvation is our truth, healing is also our truth.

The end was in sight—but the remaining month felt considerably longer than the preceding two months had. Our house was nearing completion, but we were having frequent issues preventing us from being able to officially move in. We were still in the apartment, and my daily schedule involved getting up around 8 a.m., dressing, eating, bringing Caleb to the park, fixing lunch, and coming home for an afternoon nap. I was frequently a single mom because Jason spent many late nights at the gym, where he was trying to establish himself as a credible business owner. Instead of cooking, I often enjoyed takeout through the extra income we earned from the business.

My night typically ended with a walk with Caleb, bathing him, bringing him to bed, and then watching television until my husband arrived home.

I had entered a calm state as I neared the end. A calm which didn't involve such a fierce, intense fighting anymore. I invited God into my daily activities, resting in the knowledge that his will would be done, and in this peaceful state I started to enjoy my family once again rather than viewing them as a deterrent to the maturing of my faith.

July 8, 2004

> I'm definitely feeling calm and peaceful, but I know the enemy goes about seeking whom he may kill or destroy, 1 Peter 5:8, so I'm on guard. We had our neonatal appointment yesterday, and it was a very positive experience. The doctor was uplifting and didn't even mention one negative thing. He said it was just a wait and see sort of thing, and our next ultrasound is Thursday. "Whoever [me] shall say to this mountain [of water] be removed and cast into the sea and does not doubt in his heart [by combating the enemy in our minds] but believes that those things he says will be done he will have [not maybe or conditionally] whatever he or she says" Mark 11:23.

I felt peaceful most of the time, but I do recall one night in particular where peace was nonexistent. We had decided to take a family trip to check on the status of our new house. The ride was uneventful, Jason taking the wheel and driving the few miles between the apartment and our future home. We entered the house, purely wood and drywall at this point, and as we toured the upstairs floor, Jason explained to Caleb where our bedroom was, then his bedroom, the bathroom, and the new baby's room.

When I heard those words, something inside of me snapped. I had been edgy for some time. The pregnancy was coming down to the wire, the baby was moving like a normal baby, and I was drained from being on pins and needles, wondering daily if this would be the day that I didn't feel movement anymore and my baby would be pronounced dead. As Jason pointed out the baby's room, I sarcastically said, "maybe."

Jason, in his bold, no-nonsense, ticked-off voice replied, "Yes, this will be the baby's room."

The car ride home began silently. I didn't know how to explain to my husband the relentless dread I felt every day, every hour, as I constantly waited for the next slight movement or flutter or kick indicating life. How could I express how the stress boiled over at times, and how I just wanted to live, to be present, to not live in an endless panic anymore? How, above all else, anything else, I wanted to put a baby in that bedroom?

I didn't know how to say any of it, so I sat there silently while hot tears dripped slowly down my face. I was drained. I didn't want to live in fear anymore.

Neither of us had anything profound to say, so we didn't speak. And as we each nursed our silent pains, Jason pulled into McDonald's, where we ordered an ice cream cone to soothe the wide-eyed two-year-old in the back seat, who was not moving a muscle, and who was clearly confused about Mommy and Daddy's heated conversation.

July 13, 2004

Two days until our appointment. I'm so calm and at rest. It has to be Jesus. There is absolutely no other explanation. I'm ready to meet little Lucas or Grace but not until my due date. The pregnant me is declaring a full-term pregnancy, vaginal delivery, and a total diminishing of the water. He or she is going crazy right now kicking with life. Psalm 118:17, "I will not die but live and proclaim what the Lord has done." I believe, and I'm fully confident and persuaded of that fact for this baby. The baby is healed, because the Word was sent to heal (Psalm 107); that's the Word's function. This baby is honored to have such a testimony, and I'm honored among mothers to have birthed not only a baby but a whole new level of faith.

July 16, 2004

Praise God! The hydrocephalus has stopped progressing. The water level has remained the same since June 15, and we saw a perfect profile, a healthy heart and spine, and the baby was sucking on the placenta! We have an awesome God! I'm scheduled for a C-section on August 12, and I believe "Whoever says to this mountain, be removed and be cast into the sea and does not doubt in his heart, but believes that those things he says will be done, he will have whatever he says. Therefore, I say to you, whatever things you ask when you pray, believe that you receive them and you will have them" Mark 11:23. As Smith Wigglesworth says, "Only believe." I believe and declare that God is able to and will drain this water and reduce the head size. I believe that the baby is healed mentally and physically and that the enemy's authority to kill, steal, or destroy has been demolished through Christ's victory at Calvary. This baby will be a living, breathing testimony to the glory and power of God.

July 22, 2004

Six days have passed? Wow, time is flying. Three weeks until the C-section, but the neurosurgeon wants to meet us before that day. My appointment with the neurosurgeon is on Thursday, and then it's just two weeks until the glory of God is manifested throughout the hospital. I don't worry, because any thoughts of doubt get killed immediately. Jesus is my Word, and he is life for this baby. God is good. His love endures forever. I keep praying for more faith, for God to help any unbelief, and to move this mountain of water.

God was still teaching me daily about the meaning of healing as I walked and talked with him. Before the diagnosis I would never have thought I could endure a trial like facing the death of my unborn child, but God faithfully gave me the capacity to endure and even to grow through the pain. My heart was still constantly heavy for my unborn child, but through the heaviness God reminded me of his faithfulness, and that was where the glorious part of it all came together.

I learned, painfully and slowly, that God had to come before all—even before my baby. I became willing, through faithful prayer, petition, and seeking his will above all other wills, to become like Abraham, to sacrifice my child upon the altar of faith and to trust God's perfect will above any of my brilliant ideas.

I learned the lesson eventually.

I did trust him, usually, and I did believe the child would be healed completely, most of the time. Yet, despite all my declaring and battling, I did occasionally think about what life would look like with a handicapped child, even though everything within me wanted to rebuke the devil for whispering blasphemous thoughts in my ear. I wrestled daily with the meaning of faith, true faith that speaks to a mountain and declares that this or that occur—and was that even faith, I wondered? Or was faith more of learning to trust in God's plan, that he would orchestrate everything according to his divine purpose? Less than a month away from meeting my baby, I allowed myself to sink into a blissful rest with the Lord. I walked confidently with a peaceful countenance. For the first time, I began to really understand a peace that passes understanding (Philippians 4:7).

July 27, 2004

Five more days have passed? I can't believe how quickly time is passing. God is good. He does carry our loads, and he gives rest and a complete peace that passes understanding. The baby is active, like crazy, to the point of me losing sleep, praise God! I never thought I would truly understand the meaning of walking with God, but now I daily walk with him and talk with him.

God often gets our attention through the hardships of life. Pain turns our gaze heavenward as we realize we are but mortals in desperate need of his mercy and grace upon our lives. God literally carried that heavy, cumbersome load in the final weeks. The daily kicks were such beautiful, needed reminders of life.

They were also signs of the knowledge I rested upon: life, for my child, was indeed being affirmed through every movement.

CHAPTER 9

A Final Charge

"My grace is sufficient for you, for my power is perfected in weakness."

2 Corinthians 12:9

July 29, 2004

"Resist the Devil, and he will flee from you." James 4:7

I was bombarded with doubts as we neared the end of our journey. I repeatedly spoke Scripture and rebuked the devil's attacks as random thoughts constantly plagued me. *Your baby will die, the damage is too severe, you'll be stuck raising a vegetable, your life will never be the same, you will be tied to this person who has no independence.* I struck them down one by one, rebuking them in the healing name of Jesus Christ.

This was the home stretch, and I felt like a racer eyeing the finish line. I had entered a war zone, me and the blood of Christ against the demons of hell, and I would be damned if I was going to give them one inch of the peace that passes understanding, promised to those who put their faith in the Lord (Philippians 4:7).

I knew others were standing in prayer beside me, but it felt like it was my battle—my victory or my loss—more than anyone else's. Even more than Jason's. I had bonded with the baby over the past few months, and I alone felt him or her growing under my heart. The unbreakable maternal bond had been formed, and I was not ready to let go.

July 30, 2004

Earthly fact—My baby was diagnosed with hydrocephalus and possible brain damage. God's fact—This baby is healed. "I am the Lord who heals you." Exodus 15:26

Earthly fact—My baby has water on the brain. God's fact—"Therefore I tell you, whatever you ask for in prayer, believe that you have received it, and it will be yours." Mark 11:23

Earthly fact—A baby with hydrocephalus has a high mortality rate. God's fact—"The Devil seeks to kill, steal, and destroy, but I have come to give you abundant life." John 10:10

Earthly fact—Mothers who carry babies with hydrocephalus most often have a C-section. God's fact— "Go! It will be done, just as you believed it would" (to the centurion). Matt 8:13

At my previous appointment, the doctor had informed me that I was going to have to have a C-section due to the size of the baby's head. I was dead set against this. I don't know how I thought I was going to push a baby with a two-year-old's head out of my body, but I was speaking and believing for a vaginal birth—even though the C-section was scheduled for August 12. Thank God for doctors who can make sensible decisions when crazy, hormonal mothers think they know best.

August 5, 2004

I delivered the Israelites from Pharaoh, and all they did was complain in the desert. I delivered your baby from the enemy, and all you do is complain about the pregnancy. Father, forgive me. I praise you for the aches and pains in my legs and back. I praise you for the weariness and the heartburn. I praise you because in being pregnant, I am a testimony to your Word, which says "I am the Lord your healer." Thank you for my pregnancy.

Smith Wigglesworth: "The Master does not want us to reason things out, for carnal reasoning will always land us in a bog of unbelief. He wants us to simply obey. Do not be afraid, just believe."

My legs ached whenever I moved or sat still or stood or did anything during the last seven days before the C-section. My nerves were the same. I felt as if someone had lit them on fire and thrown them around the yard for a Fourth of July spectacle, and I was emotionally and physically drained. Every thought throughout each twenty-four-hour period was a battle as I willed my body to continue and willed my mind to stay strong.

I wanted to feel relaxed, to feel some relief from the constant praying, reading, rebuking, and growing my faith, but instead weariness began to overshadow the peace during those final days.

One night I had a dream. In this dream, I walked into heaven and saw Jesus rocking a tiny baby. The baby had a large, oversized head and was wrapped completely in white swaddling clothes. I stood in the dream, mesmerized, as I gazed upon my heavenly Father caring for that frail baby, and my heart grasped what the dream was really about. Jesus not only cared for my baby, but he also cared deeply for me.

When I awoke, the vision remained and I wept. *Wow! Jesus cared not only for my baby but he deeply cared for me—a screwed-up, emotionally fragile mother whom he knew needed some peace in these final days.*

My body was racked with sobs of love for my Savior over the gift he had given me in the dream. That dream brought an incredible amount of comfort in those final days.

August 7, 2004

Hebrews 4—Perfect rest is an obedience and trust in God, not in human works. Just as salvation is of the grace of God, so is healing.

August 11, 2004

This is the night before my scheduled C-section. I'm not nervous, just excited and anxious about being a mom of two children. I've read and reread Isaiah 35 about God's peace in times like these. I fully believe that baby Lucas or Grace is healed; nothing missing, nothing broken. I know that God's glory will shine down, and many will know that he is the Lord God Almighty. This baby will not die but live and declare his works. I believe my baby will live a long, abundant life with complete wholeness mentally and physically.

Jason wrote this: I believe in my heart that God has healed our baby. I'm anxious for tomorrow and cannot wait to see God's glory shining down in front of those doctors. "Everything is possible for him who believes" Mark 9:23.

Late that night, Jason and I lay in bed sharing our amazement that the big moment we had been waiting for was upon us. We were lighthearted, but this feeling was tempered with the desperate hope that we were not in for a day of complete despair. I teetered between faith and wondering if I was in so much denial that I couldn't even see the truth anymore. I repeatedly went there—to the worst-case scenario, which was being handed a dead baby, or worse yet, being handed a live baby who would die moments or hours after I had bonded with him or her. I slept restlessly, fidgeting often throughout the night due to nerves, discomfort, and hormones.

The next morning, the two of us quietly dressed. A somber stillness hung heavily in the air as we contemplated the coming day. We pulled into the hospital parking garage and prayed before exiting the car, "Father, thy will be done, on earth as it is in heaven." And then we walked, silently, hand in hand into the hospital to face the final leg of our journey.

As I wobbled, I braced my heavy body against Jason, who had more emotional and physical strength to offer. I had felt the baby moving and kicking throughout the night, so I was confident I would be delivering a live baby, but beyond that, I was completely ignorant as to what the day might hold.

CHAPTER 10

Victory!

*"But for you who revere my name the Son of Righteousness
will rise with healing in his wings."*

Malachi 4:2

Our baby arrived early in the afternoon on August 12, 2004. As the tiny body was aggressively lifted out of my stomach, Jason roared with laughter and yelled, "It's a boy!" It had to be a boy. Lucas Aaron had made his arrival.

And I finally exhaled, breathing out months of stress, anticipation, fear, and hope. As they slowly exited my body, I quietly whispered, "Thank you, Jesus," and then let body and soul sink into a calm I had not felt in a long time.

Through my drug-induced haze, I overheard some scattered information: healthy boy, seven pounds, ten ounces, Apgar score—a simple method to quickly access the health of a baby—of seven. Five minutes later that same score became a nine. I thought, *Wow! A nine at five minutes, and this was a baby declared dead only months earlier?* I couldn't comprehend it.

I lay there dizzy with awe as many hands worked to stitch up my belly, which had been cut open from one end to the other in order to accommodate a two-year-old-sized head, and many more hands worked on the delicate baby boy. I lay silent, soaking in the moment and anxiously stealing glances at my beautiful little boy as he continuously wailed hearty screams of life. I watched as the nurses took his vitals, and I marveled at how normal he seemed—crying, kicking, flailing his arms, just like Caleb had at birth.

In that instant my body, overwhelmed with the gravity of the moment, began shaking. Shaking from the epidural, shaking from fear of the still unknown, and shaking from having my heart ripped out of my body.

Despite my fears, Lucas passed all of his initial tests and was whisked off to neonatal, where he would be attached to monitors in preparation for a shunt surgery in the coming days.

As I watched him disappear from sight, loneliness descended. I achingly wanted my baby but knew I could not have him. I lay there, not knowing who was taking care of him and having every cell in my body scream, "I am his mama! I need to take care of him!" even though I knew I didn't possess the knowledge or the energy to care for a child with his medical needs in those moments.

Over the next few days I slowly recuperated. I pumped excessive amounts of breast milk, because I was convinced he had to have my milk for his brain development. I was wheeled or assisted down to neonatal multiple times a day, where I sat for hours rocking him and singing "Jesus Loves Me" and "Amazing Grace."

As I rocked him, he would often squint his eyes as if he were in extreme pain. We were told that he did this before he was shunted because the fluid buildup in his brain caused intense, migraine-like headaches. He was administered around-the-clock medications to help ease the pain, but I was aware it did not completely alleviate the pressure he felt in his head.

Jason and I were taught how to care for Lucas. One technique was especially difficult to master: gavage feeding (inserting a feeding tube down the baby's nostril). As a mother I hated doing it, especially because Lucas had the ability to nurse and to take a bottle, but we had to know how to perform the procedure in case he stopped sucking. Shoving a tube down our baby boy's nostril was emotionally painful, as we were informed that if the tube did not go in correctly, we could drown Lucas's lungs with fluid.

Thankfully, we never had to go that route once we were home, but the experience led me to research the possibility of creating a gavage doll, a tool parents could practice on rather than having to use their own child. Apparently another person had a similar idea; when I looked into it, I learned it had already been created.

An area volunteer group faithfully made quilts for NICU babies, and Lucas soon had a big, beautiful Noah's ark quilt hanging above his crib as a symbol of God's constant faithfulness in the most hopeless of situations. He was also given a little blue lamb that played "Jesus Loves Me," and he would lay, eyes wide with wonder, listening to this beautiful music from his little lamb.

I would daily rock my miracle boy and dwell on the journey I had been through to finally arrive at this moment where my child was no longer in my womb but instead thriving in my arms.

Faced with the reality of Lucas's condition and freed from the need to keep fighting, I worked through the false perception I'd held through the past few months that God acts as a magician on our behalf when we use our "speak it and believe it" theologies. I came to the realization that God requires obedience, regardless of the outcome of our trials, and faith is not spending every moment reading the Bible, praying, and chanting faith-based words to procure a specific outcome. There is a season for these actions, but there is a season for being the hands and feet of Christ as well, getting in the muck of life and feeling it, living it, being in the moments.

A wise man I know, who also went through tragic life circumstances, says, "When Jesus is your Lord, he is in everything—the small, the mediocre, the big stuff. He is in making spaghetti, taking the kids to school, making love to your spouse, painting the dining room a different color, planting a garden, changing diapers, and rocking your newborn baby."

Being a follower of Jesus Christ requires being in all of the messiness of life and letting our light shine in all circumstances. That's faith. That's stepping away from the appearance of holiness and becoming truly holy. That's what Christ wants to do in our lives.

Ultimately, the pain, the struggles, the negotiations taught me that I was not in control, not one single bit. My faith became a complete surrender to God's will and had absolutely nothing to do with any of my actions. I learned to trust in a will that was beyond anything my human comprehension could ever grasp.

* * *

Jason and I continued to attend numerous meetings with doctors, in which we were dumbfounded as we listened to the same specialists who had declared death for our baby for so long now declaring life as they related how our little boy should be just fine.

And he *was* fine. He had a heavenly Father who had watched over him from the day he was created and surrounded him with a host of angels tending to his every breath.

August 19, 2004

Baby Lucas is one week today. He is beautiful. My little heartbeat. God's blessing and God's greatest teacher to me, and the biggest roller-coaster ride ever. I have my little boy playing baseball.

Thursday went well. The C-section was at 1:30, and Lucas was born at 2:00. The doctor asked Jason what the sex was, he said a boy, and I bawled. He had to be a boy. He came out kicking and crying. The C-section was much less painful than Caleb's birth. They rushed him to neonatal where we went to see him an hour later. The next few days were a blur.

He acts like a normal baby, and he looks like a normal baby except for his head size which is forty-five cm. He grasped our fingers, kicked his legs, all of his organs were perfect, and he nursed. We were told that 20 percent of his head was brain due to the fluid buildup, and the neurosurgeon suggested shunting. He was highly optimistic that Lucas's strength would aid him in a successful surgery outcome. Tuesday at 3 p.m. he went in to be shunted. He was bathed in prayers. I felt angels all around his bed as he was wheeled in, and I begged God to let me see one, but I didn't. The presence of angels was overwhelming to me.

His nurse, Nancy, has been an angel in human form to us. She is wonderful. She prayed for him before he went into surgery. Jason and I prayed for two hours that he would remain stable. His surgery was finished at 5:30, and the neurosurgeon came out smiling while Lucas came out with his eyes wide open. He was so beautiful.

The surgery went very well, and he's been monitored for the past two days. His head is down to forty-three, and he nursed again today. He is grasping harder, lifting both hands to his mouth and being my sweet boy. The nurses talked for the first time about bringing him home in a few days. God's grace is sufficient, and his power is perfected in weakness. In my weakness he fills in the spots with power. In Lucas's weaknesses, he faithfully fills in with power. His Word is absolute truth and life for those who reach out in faith and take it. Lucas's nurse said the sweetest thing the other day: "I believe that God gives very special babies to very special parents." That made my day. God is good and faithful, and he will continue to give grace on this new journey with Lucas.

I was discharged from the hospital on August 15 and was home for a week and a half without my baby, so I pumped as much breast milk as humanly possible and brought vials of the substance to the nurse's station. They laughed and added the additions to the already large stash stored in the refrigerator labeled "Baby Crisman."

Pumping gave me a purpose, a tangible way to take care of my baby without physically being at the hospital. I visited Lucas in the mornings with Caleb and again later in the evenings when Jason came home. I felt lonely and guilty without my baby, guilty over not being able to take care of him and somewhat embarrassed about that reality.

Normal mothers had the instinctual ability to care for their babies, and here I was, the oldest of twelve, a former nanny, mother of a two-year-old, and I wasn't physically capable of caring for my newborn. Normal mothers carried a baby for nine months and then immediately carried that baby in their arms for the following months, but my arms felt heavy and empty, like dead weights hanging limply at my sides, serving no purpose. The guilt arrived fresh each morning, with each restful night of sleep that I enjoyed because I had not awakened to a baby's cries, with professionals caring for him across town.

Following Lucas's birth, Jason proudly hung a baby announcement at his gym, along with a synopsis of our testimony below it:

> Doctors said he would die before birth and suggested abortion. They said there was nothing they could do to save him. Then they said he would die in our arms. Then they said he would die during surgery. Then they said he would not be able to see or hear. Now they can't explain why he is alive and seeing and hearing. Trust not in the wisdom of men but rather in the power of God!

Those who saw this testimony were moved to tears: a strong, personal trainer and gym owner, acknowledging that the God of the universe had just healed his baby boy. For Jason, as for me, it had been a battle and a journey of faith. Now, even with the challenges that remained, we exulted in victory.

CHAPTER 11

A False Rest

"For the Lord loves the just and will not forsake
his faithful ones."

Psalm 37:28

August 29, 2004

Tomorrow Lucas comes home. He is doing very well. He passed
a hearing test today, and he's nursing and bottle feeding. God is
so faithful. Lucas is seventeen days old and thriving. I've learned
to stop trying and start trusting God, especially when it comes to
my family. All I can do is pray and believe for God's protection
around each one of them and go from there. I refuse to allow
fear to run my life. I believe that Lucas is completely healed. I
believe that the pressure is gone. I believe that his shunt operates in complete perfection. I believe that Jesus is the author and
finisher of his life, and I believe that every cell, tissue, neuron,
system, organ, bone, and joint in his body operates in complete
wholeness in Jesus's name.

I woke up bright and early on this day, elated to be bringing my
baby boy home. Any fear of the unknown was completely masked
by elatedness. We went as a family to bring Lucas home, and when
we arrived he was officially detached from all lifesaving equipment.
He was bathed, dressed, and placed ever so delicately into his car
seat. We pulled away from the hospital with seven pages of discharge

papers, and when we arrived home I went through every page and circled each word I did not completely understand. Later that night, I would get online and research terms like *cerebral dysgenesis, septum pellucidum,* and *dysplastic corpus callosum* until I understood precisely what the professionals were saying about my child.

Lucas left the hospital free of medications, free of allergies, and free of any problems other than a shunt we were told to keep a vigilant eye on. We pulled into our apartment complex, and I held tightly to the car seat holding my miracle baby. This moment was the epitome of everything I had prayed for. I was home, Lucas was home, my family was home. Praise the Lord.

August 30, 2004

My baby is home, praise the Lord oh my soul! God is faithful to his redeemed, and there is a highway for us where no lion shall trespass and everlasting joy and gladness shall be upon them (Isaiah 35). A beautiful promise for those whose hope is in the Lord. Lucas is a joy, an absolute beauty to behold. God has healed him completely, and that is our everlasting testimony. I'm tired now, very tired, and I have a long night with my beautiful baby boy. Good night and God bless.

I wrote the words with joy and a sense of closure. It would be my last entry—I thought. The journey was over.

Isaiah 35 had comforted my fears as I birthed Lucas, watched him struggle, watched him thrive, watched him overcome all odds placed against his life, watched him undergo surgery at three days old, and finally watched him become part of the Crisman family.

Although there was immense joy in bringing our baby home, those first few months were also extremely trying. Lucas had to be watched constantly due to his head size. He slept in a bassinet next to our bed, so Jason and I got very little sleep, never having the luxury of a deep sleep. Lucas slept on his back, and if he were to flip over in the night, he would be unable to lift his face out of the mattress.

The fear kept me awake most nights, my mind racing in the darkest hours, wondering if I had brought a baby home only to have him die of suffocation in the midnight hour. There were many nights I would awaken, notice his head turned one way or the other with his face slightly buried in the mattress, and for a moment would believe he had died. I lived in a world that was constantly teetering between faith and despair.

Only a week into our homecoming, Lucas started passing crystal-like bowel movements. I frantically called the doctor, who told me to feed him a bottle immediately because he was severely dehydrated. I didn't understand. Lucas had been nursing, I thought, and I had continued to supplement with bottles. I immediately set up an appointment for the following day with a lactation consultant. As I spoke with her and demonstrated Lucas's nursing ability for her, she confirmed that yes, it appeared as if he were sucking, but looks were deceiving. Lucas was not ingesting any milk through his sucks, and this had been going on for days, with only the daily supplementation of a small bottle or two! I felt like a complete failure as a mother.

Our life felt overwhelming, and the angst only continued to rise with the construction of a new house, taking care of a family, and building a business.

When Lucas was only a few weeks old, Caleb, who was two years old at the time, seemed to be feeling the stress of a new sibling. One day he decided that his baby brother was bothering him and slapped him square across the face. Lucas only moaned quietly.

On the one hand I couldn't believe Caleb was capable of such a cruel action, but on the other hand, I completely understood his anger and frustration toward his new baby brother. I had moments where I thought, *This is so hard. Why in the world would I have prayed to have this child?* Moments later I would feel waves of guilt over having such a horrible thought.

In time, Lucas became our reality; a reality we often made modifications for, but our reality nonetheless. We put his car seat in the front passenger seat rather than the usual place in the back middle after a heart-stopping incident while taking the boys out one afternoon. Our destination was about ten miles away. We loaded into the car, both children in the back seat, and departed. Upon our arrival I circled around to Lucas's car seat and discovered he was nearly suffocating himself! His head had fallen forward, dangerously low upon his neck, and he was unable to lift it back up!

I cradled him gently, tears again streaming down my face, thinking, *How in the world am I going to keep this child alive? Why would God give me such a delicate creature?* Even in all of my fitful moments of questioning and despair, God remained steadfast, always providing enough wisdom moment by moment.

Jason and I were on edge for those first few months, concerned that every little thing could be a shunt problem or some other undiagnosed issue.

A few weeks into being home, we had a routine appointment with the neurologist to review Lucas's recent MRI results. We glowed with pride as the neurologist exhibited the scans on a big blackboard and explained that most of the fluid had disappeared and been replaced with brain matter. He displayed an element of lackluster surprise as the pictures revealed that the ventricles seemed to have decreased in size, "not a normal occurrence," in his words. Jason, not one to mince words, declared, "God healed him!" The stoic-faced neurologist snickered, but we didn't care, and we actually snickered back, confident that "our faith rested not on the knowledge of men but on the power of God."

In December of 2004, we finally moved into our dream house, four months after Lucas was born. We naïvely believed the expanded space would remedy many of our problems—problems such as the tight quarters apartment living offered and the lack of space for the two boys.

Lucas would eventually need his own bedroom, Caleb was a stir-crazy two-year-old with nowhere to roam in our third-story apartment, and Jason had a grand idea for a sword room to house his beloved collection from around the world. Unfortunately, the move was not a magic cure. I continued to monitor Lucas throughout the night by having him sleep in a small bassinet beside our bed. He couldn't roll from side to side like a normal baby, so the setup didn't pose any additional risks. He still did not sleep well, waking up throughout the night with grunts and noises that always had the ability to startle me. We reluctantly moved him to a regular crib around six months old and trusted that heavenly angels would surround him and keep watch throughout the night. I quit nursing early on, but I was determined to pump throughout his infancy because I still thoroughly believed that he needed breast milk for brain development.

Lucas spent the majority of his first year lying on his back, unable to hold his head up, and because of this position, his head began to resemble a flat pancake. The specialist recommended a reshaping helmet that Lucas absolutely hated. The physician's instructions called for only a few months of constant wear, breaking for an hour a day to bathe, but I ignored the instructions. I felt incredibly sorry for my child with his oversized, sopping wet head, dripping with sweat throughout the hot summers of Michigan. With the already exhausting sleeping issues we were dealing with on a daily basis, I couldn't be coerced into adding this corrective device to our nightly misery. However, by ignoring the original instructions which called for almost constant wear, I ultimately doomed my child to twelve months of misery instead of what should have been only a few months.

We hoped Lucas's sleep problems would resolve on their own, but for three years he continued to wake up most nights. He would bang his head and scream, making it impossible for us to sleep, and we had no idea what the problem was.

Around his fourth birthday, I made an appointment for Lucas to be seen at a pediatric sleep clinic. He and Jason checked in for the night, Lucas comfortable in the crib while attached to numerous monitors and cords; Jason uncomfortable in the reclining chair beside him. There was high anticipation all around; we were excited for any answers we were finally going to receive when the tests came back in the morning. The tests did come back, bright and early, and they showed . . . absolutely nothing, a frustrating verdict. Without a problem there was no solution, and we were forced back to square one.

Lucas continued to wake up periodically throughout the night and scream, head banging for no apparent reason until, finally exhausted, he fell back to sleep. His grandma jokingly suggested we add a little whiskey to his bottle, like they did in the olden days. We considered the idea, but only for a moment, out of desperation to engage in this elusive thing known to the rest of the world as sleep.

CHAPTER 12

Lucas Life:
The First Year and Beyond

"He is the faithful God."

Deuteronomy 7:9

Lucas's first birthday was a monumental milestone. We were amazed that we had somehow kept this special little boy alive for a whole year, and not only alive, but thriving! Friends and family were invited to a birthday celebration in his honor.

When the day arrived, he was recovering from yet another ear infection and his first case of pink eye. The ear infections were an ongoing battle, causing repeated suffering (on his part and ours) until we finally resorted to a tubal procedure around his fifth birthday. In the process, we finally found a few answers for his sleep problems. Many of these nightly issues we discovered were a direct result of the ear infections. Banging his head and screaming uncontrollably became ominous signs that his ear was hurting, and that, in turn, immediately signaled it was time to bring him to the doctor.

Through all these months we remained on a constant lookout for a shunt malfunction, having been informed that most children with shunts have repeated problems with these devices when they either become clogged or don't adapt positively to the individual's body. We prominently hung on our refrigerator a detailed list of all of the possible symptoms. Unfortunately, these symptoms could describe nearly any childhood illness and included vomiting, diarrhea, screaming, and head banging. One symptom stood out above the rest, though, and it became the symptom that eventually did land us in the emergency room—extreme sleepiness and lifelessness.

One morning, when Lucas was a little past one year old, after a difficult evening of monitoring him yet again for some unknown ailment, we were unable to awaken him. I lifted him gently from the crib, but his body was limp and not responding to anything we said or did. My mind immediately went to the worst-case scenario. *He was dying.*

I frantically called the family doctor, who encouraged us to come in immediately. He took one look at Lucas and said, "You have a very sick little boy. Get him to the ER."

Jason and I paced the hospital hallway while Lucas underwent hours of tests. The final prognosis was that Lucas had his first shunt malfunction. We felt strangely relieved to finally have this watched-for event transpire, for now we were familiar with the symptoms, and we were also comfortable with the solution and the recovery process.

Ironically, in the process of this scare, I became elevated in the medical community's estimation. The doctors suddenly viewed me as an expert when it came to my child's care. They recognized that I, his mother, understood his needs more thoroughly than they ever could, and my voice became not only highly valued and respected but trumped all other opinions. After years of feeling like I had no valuable opinion or options and instead had to blindly follow what the experts deemed necessary for my child, my flesh and blood, I loved being viewed as the ultimate authority. I felt like I had earned that respect and was happy to accept the role.

The shunt was replaced during a surgery that was less dramatic than all of the surrounding apprehension. Immediately after surgery, Lucas was groggy but alert. He remained hospitalized for three days to monitor his recovery, a treasured time of respite for a tired mom who rarely received a full night's sleep. I felt guilty over leaving my baby boy at the hospital and felt (justly or unjustly) judged by the nursing staff, but I desperately needed those nights of complete rest and regrouping. Lucas was left with hugs, kisses, his "Jesus Loves Me" lamb, and his beloved green blanket. I called before bedtime, the staff assured me that he was doing well, and then I slept deeply for the first time in months.

Two years later, after visiting with a local physical therapist, I smiled to read the report we were sent home with. "His past medical history is remarkable for hydrocephalus. He was shunted at the age of about three days. He was born at thirty-six weeks and was in the NICU for two weeks. He has had only one shunt revision." Remarkable indeed.

Lucas continued to gain strength through interactions with family as well as through a local Early On program, which was free for parents of special needs children and involved weekly individual attention with physical and occupational therapists. These interactions with dedicated specialists significantly assisted his development. He sat independently at sixteen months and crawled at twenty. His crawl was a sight to behold. With limited neck strength, his head was still too heavy for him to hold up consistently, but he was determined to get from one place to another. His unique situation involved dragging his oversized head forward along the ground. After a few weeks of this, he acquired a noticeable bald spot where his hair repeatedly came in contact with the carpet. His efforts were inspiring.

Later that year, one of the megachurches in the area heard about our story and asked if they could use it as the cover story in the upcoming church newsletter. We eagerly agreed, wanting anyone who could be touched by Lucas's story to be able to read it. They ran the story in the fall of 2005, and the outpouring of gratitude and support was overwhelming. The large-scale recognition of God's faithfulness made us realize again that everything was driven by a purpose and worth enduring if people could be touched by our hardships.

Lucas continued to provide us with daily surprises as he grew, and with the surprises came routine scares as well. One heart-stopping incident occurred after we put him to bed in a real crib around the age of one. Jason and I had settled in for the night when we heard a loud thump. I ran to Lucas's room to discover a scene that left me speechless: my baby was lying on the floor, on his back, looking up at me with a big smile! Somehow he had managed to stand in his crib and lurch his fragile body over the rail. I could not believe it!

He seemed completely unfazed and just looked at me with a big, goofy smile. I grabbed him, and in stunned silence, I gently held his frail body and big head, beside myself with fear, thinking that he might have caused internal damage or hurt his head or even his shunt. His pain tolerance has always been a mystery. He has never shed a tear; instead he screams, which leads to a guessing game. Is he screaming out of anger? Boredom? Pain? No one ever really knows for sure.

After Lucas successfully overcame the "he will never live" prognosis, the doctors declared a new doom-and-gloom report. The new prognosis read "he will never see or walk," but my faith knew he was going to play baseball someday—a skill that would require both sight and the ability to be ambulatory.

Around the same time, at about eighteen months old, Lucas also discovered an entertaining new hobby which seemed to occupy him for hours. He would put his fingers deep into his right eye and play with it. He smiled, big goofy smiles, as he dug his finger around and felt the squishiness. To stop him, we tied his hands in socks and constantly swatted his fingers away, but he would only sway his head back and forth, smiling, thinking we were playing a game, and go right back to digging.

We made an appointment at the best pediatric opthamologist we could find. She examined his eye and concluded that he had destroyed his cornea and would one day, in all likelihood, need a cornea transplant. But for the time being, seeing that he wouldn't and couldn't wear glasses, we just had to live with what had occurred and do our best to prevent any further damage.

Lucas has always loved videos. The bright sights and sounds would mesmerize him. He also loved music, any kind of music, and would sing along with many songs.

One day, as seven-month-old Lucas watched one of these music videos, I began to wonder if he knew about his feet. I wasn't sure he could see far enough to be aware of the appendages at the bottom of his legs, but he was extremely flexible, so I lifted one thin leg up to his face and showed him the small foot attached to his ankle. Immediately, he was curious and reached out to grab it—the beginning of a new favorite hobby of his.

Around this time, I also began experimenting with baby food for him, and although he wasn't particularly fond of anything green, he did love pears and applesauce. As he progressed to other foods and eventually ate what we were eating around the age of two, he came up with a unique demand: anything that went into his mouth had to have peanut butter on it. He would not eat anything—spinach, bread, pizza, anything—unless it was smothered in peanut butter. If it was not, it was immediately thrown to the floor.

Lack of sleep—mine, Jason's, and Lucas's—continued to be a trying ordeal for the whole family. We experimented with melatonin, at Lucas's doctor's suggestion, adding higher dosages than normal. This natural remedy provided some relief. Lucas's nighttime awakenings went from four or five times a night to two or three. Our second sleep solution arrived through a state-funded full-size bed, padded with six-foot-tall walls that safely and totally enclosed Lucas, keeping him completely secure throughout the night. And finally, we moved him to the first floor while we maintained some distance a floor above in the master bedroom. This move provided occasional relief from the ear-piercing screams as Jason and I grew accustomed to the quiet whirl of the fan near our bed, drowning out any additional grunts or groans.

By the time Lucas was two, we had surpassed most of the major hurdles: head issues, sleep issues, eating issues, helmet issues, and one shunt malfunction issue. We had finally settled into a new normal as a family of four.

It was by the grace of God we survived those first few years.

In 2008, at a routine physical therapy appointment, we were overjoyed to read on Lucas's checkout report these words: "Statistically speaking, a young man who is doing this well at the age of 3.5 is almost certain to be able to ambulate on his own, perhaps with assistive devices and with continued support."

In other words, our boy would walk one day.

God was faithful, and he remained faithful as the dust settled on one journey while another, even more difficult in many ways, was quickly gaining momentum right around the bend.

CHAPTER 13

Another Storm

"He took up our infirmities and carried our diseases."

Matthew 8:17

Mabel Grace, our sweet little princess girl, was born on February 26, 2007. I was overjoyed to have a girl after two boys. I became the primary caregiver for our new infant, and the responsibility for Lucas's care became Jason's daily task. The innate busyness of caring for our children began to innocently creep into our lives, and a crack slowly started to weave its destruction through our marriage.

I stopped sleeping in our bed and instead slept beside Mabel in the nursery. Jason and I justified the arrangement as a survival tactic. In reality, the change was a way for me to distance myself from a husband, who was starting to have a plethora of unexplained health problems, including an almost nonexistent libido. There were times when I even questioned his fidelity, an absurd idea—but I had no other explanation for the change in his behavior. I didn't push this accusation too aggressively, not exactly wanting to encourage any extracurricular activities, as I was already completely exhausted.

The new arrangement was successful, at least for a time, as it allowed everyone in the family to obtain as much rest as possible. However, in the process of dividing and conquering, I also began distancing myself from Lucas, a move that would be problematic in the months and years to come.

Jason's health continued to inexplicably deteriorate, with high blood sugar issues, dizziness, weight loss, and increased disorientation. Two different specialists diagnosed him with type 1 diabetes, a diagnosis riddled with confusion, considering he was the epitome of health, employed as a personal trainer and tennis professional. I remained preoccupied with our newborn and didn't concern myself too obsessively with his health problems, feeling instead that he was capable of managing the prognosis on his own with his education and training.

Financial worries loomed as well. Hushed discussions involving Jason and his partner indicated that one of them should gracefully bow out of ownership in the fitness industry. Jason stubbornly charged forward during an economic downturn, not willing to abandon his first baby, the gym, and we began a descent into personal financial ruin. He worked without receiving a paycheck for more than six months because there simply wasn't any money. We cashed out our investments, took out a home refinance loan, and I began looking for a job, eventually finding part-time work as an after-school director.

These were not pleasant times in the Crisman household. I blamed Jason for the lack of income, while his health continued to deteriorate regardless of what he tried to do to improve it. I became resentful that I had to find a job only weeks after giving birth to our daughter, that Lucas was still severely handicapped, and that our marriage was in a deep valley from an intimacy drought. I focused on being a functioning mom, getting enough sleep, and trying to keep our family financially afloat until Jason could get his health under control. That was what we held out for: getting some concrete answers about his health. Beyond that, we hoped the rest would eventually fall into place—job, marriage, family, and intimacy, all seemingly related to getting his blood sugar numbers steady.

One unusually muggy summer night toward the end of August, I mentioned to Jason that I needed to visit my dad across town. I asked if he was feeling well enough to watch Caleb, Lucas, and Mabel, and he convinced me he felt fine. I drove twenty minutes, nervous about leaving him alone with the kids, but I reassured myself that his diagnosis was "just diabetes." Other diabetics successfully managed their sugar levels, and Jason could as well.

I pulled into my dad's driveway, and my cell phone rang. I picked it up and heard a frantic, raspy voice say, "Jess, call 911."

The phone went dead, and I went numb. I grasped the phone with white knuckles and managed to punch in the numbers, sputtering out the words to the operator on the other end: "My husband just passed out at home!" Frantic tears ran down my face.

Somehow I stumbled out of the car and burst through my dad's front door. "Jason just called and told me to call 911!" Dad returned my hysterical look with blank shock as I screamed, "I need to go home!"

Quickly I started to walk toward the car. Then Dad's brain reignited, and he insisted that I couldn't drive. After I agreed, he offered my eighty-year-old grandfather's assistance to take me home, since Dad needed to watch my younger brother and sister. All the way home, I felt like I was riding a turtle. What should have taken at most twenty minutes took closer to thirty-five but felt like an eternity.

A million thoughts flooded my mind: Was Lucas okay? What had happened? Was Jason okay? How about baby Mabel? Was he holding her when he passed out? Did he drop her? How was Caleb holding up? My little guy who had already been through way too much turmoil in his short life here on earth!

As my grandfather and I pulled into my peaceful, suburban neighborhood, we were greeted by the onslaught of sights and sounds that signaled police cars, fire trucks, and an ambulance. I rushed inside, dizzy with emotion, steadying myself against the hallway wall as I was met immediately by an assortment of paramedics, police officers, and firemen.

Within the next five minutes I learned that Jason had become disoriented and started to feel faint, and in that moment, he'd had just enough sense to quickly call me. He'd hung up the phone, proceeded to have a seizure, and passed out on our deck. The kids were, thankfully, all emotionally and physically intact. Caleb was mesmerized by the toy truck one of the firemen had given him; Mabel was safely bouncing in her ExerSaucer; and Lucas was watching a video.

The night was young, but I felt like I had just aged a million years. I would age considerably in numerous ways before the sun came up; I would never be the same again.

Someone watched the kids that night. I have no recollection of who. I remember following an ambulance in our minivan. I remember my mind being a blur of emotions, teetering between *It's just diabetes, and we'll get this under control* and the complete panic of *He is going to die.* I remember being really concerned, almost obsessed, about nursing six-month-old Mabel, who still received her nutrition primarily from my body. I remember sitting in a cold plastic chair at the hospital while my unconscious husband was wheeled from the ambulance into his hospital room.

I remember Jason going from complete unconsciousness to waking and grasping his head with both hands, moaning with inexplicable pain as he mumbled scattered words about his blood sugar. It reminded me of how Lucas had winced at birth, scrunching up his forehead, unable to explain the pain due to the fluid buildup in his head.

Various medical professionals settled Jason in his bed, started an IV, and hammered me with question after question. I felt confused and bewildered, grappling for answers as I sought to recall the details of the previous months.

When the questions stopped, I asked the one that had plagued me for months: "Why does my healthy husband have so many ailments?"

Then, finally, the young physician assistant looked me straight in the eyes and said in a voice laced with reluctance, "We're going to run an MRI to confirm that it is not a brain tumor."

It all clicked. A flood of memories attacked, washing like a tidal wave, blasting one against the other, of the past few months: the disorientation, the confusion, the vision problems, the memory problems, the weight loss, the loss of energy, the loss of libido, the sleepiness. The *lifelessness.*

"Oh, dear God. No!" I knew, in that moment, that Jason had a brain tumor. The months and days of trouble finally made sense. Diabetes had never added up, but no one had connected the dots until now. The seizure absolutely confirmed it for me.

I braced myself against the hallway wall and then slowly sank to the floor, shaking where I landed and beginning to cry. My younger sister, Hannah, wrapped her arms around my shoulders. She had come to lend moral support and brought Mabel to me so that I could nurse. I shook my head, over and over. My eyes roamed the hallway for an answer. *Please someone tell me this is a joke. Please, don't look at me that way as you pass by.* Eyes of various medical professionals glanced in pity at the young mother who had just received the news that her husband had a brain tumor. I was sure he was going to die and leave me with three young children. I would be yet another statistic, first with Lucas and now as a young widow. I had the severely handicapped child when I was young and healthy, and now I was the wife to a young, healthy husband who was going to die.

Why God? I thought. *Why do I get all the crap of the world heaped upon my shoulders? What have I done? Why can't I be a normal mom, with normal children and a normal husband who doesn't have a brain tumor in his head? Why can't we lead a normal, boring life like everyone else does? Why does it have to be so hard?*

The MRI confirmed what I already knew. The brain tumor was the size of a baseball. Jason was rushed to another local hospital and prepped for surgery. I checked into a nearby hotel with my sister and baby Mabel, which would allow me to go back and forth between the hospital for updates and the hotel to nurse the baby. I remember very few details from that long night, but I remember being tired. Not that this was out of the ordinary.

At some point during the following morning, I did make it home with Mabel to steal a few hours of coveted sleep while someone watched Caleb and Lucas. I returned to the hospital that afternoon, torn yet again between my husband and the kids.

I felt like I was failing everyone most of the time during Jason's hospital stay. On the one hand, I felt compelled to stay by Jason's side during those difficult days. On the other hand, the reality of my nursing baby called every few hours through my leaking milk ducts, and the matter of having two other children constantly tugged at my heart. I generally catered to the kids' needs, feeling incapable of doing anything constructive for my husband as he lay in a hospital bed. I never knew where I needed to be, and I struggled daily with guilt over not being physically there for him and not being emotionally available for my children. When I was physically home with the kids, my mind was a million miles away at the hospital; and when I was physically in the hospital with Jason, I worried about how the kids were coping with whoever was watching them.

The next day Jason underwent a successful surgery. The doctors were able to remove all of the visible tumor, and he was given clearance to go home three days later. The biopsy came back confirming a benign, stage 2, noncancerous tumor. We were informed that these tumors often eventually return, but there was no telling when or where this would occur, the possibility even being as far out as twenty or thirty years.

That was what we adamantly believed and hoped for—twenty or thirty years before we would have to deal with this literal headache once again. We opted to watch and wait, meaning we would not pursue chemotherapy or radiation.

In the meantime, we tried to maintain some semblance of normal in our life and for our family, although that task would become increasingly difficult as the months continued forward.

CHAPTER 14

A Miracle in the Midst of Hell

*"Do not worry about tomorrow, for tomorrow
will worry about itself."*

Matthew 6:34

Jason rebounded quickly, bursting with life and energy. With the tumor gone he became a new man overnight. He reluctantly walked away from the gym after realizing that he could not provide for his family without a steady paycheck. Instead, he found two part-time jobs. One opportunity was with a local naturopathic doctor, where he stocked nutritional products. The second was teaching tennis at a local fitness club. I continued as an after-school director, and although we were still living paycheck to paycheck, I breathed a sigh of relief that there was any paycheck at all to cash at the end of each month.

Our bills were paid, and Medicaid covered our health care. I repeatedly tried to convince Jason that we should pursue more government assistance, such as help with utility bills and food, but he would not allow it. His pride ruled out the entire concept. I shopped sparingly, clipped coupons, grew fruits and vegetables, and preserved our produce through freezing. Life was simple and beautiful, and we rested in the belief that we would not have to deal with the tumor again.

As the cooler weather crept into our peaceful neighborhood, the leaves turned beautiful colors, and we enjoyed a few months of bliss.

Then slowly and unexpectedly, the aftereffects of a tumor and brain surgery reared their ugly nature. A sudden seizure while teaching tennis resulted in immediate termination from his second job. At home, I noticed an absentmindedness from him and an inability to concentrate or remember items of importance.

With the economy bottoming out in Michigan, we lived in an extremely competitive employment climate, which often made opportunities difficult to find. Jason began work as a substitute teacher with a local school district, at the urban high school that other substitute teachers avoided, and he continued working at the doctor's office part-time.

In February, we decided that piecing together multiple jobs was not how we ultimately wanted to live, so we took a leap of faith, and Jason applied for a coveted position as a head personal trainer in Washington, DC. We had nothing to lose. We hired a babysitter for Lucas and Mabel, loaded six-year-old Caleb into the car, and trekked eight hours to DC for what we hoped could be a new beginning. This trip *would* be a new beginning, a beginning with monumental layers of grief and joy, but for reasons very different than either one of us could have predicted.

We stopped at the halfway marker in Cleveland, Ohio, and slept at a cheap hotel for the night. Caleb fell asleep quickly, exhausted from the day of traveling, and as Jason and I listened to our small child's steady breath, we seized a rare, quiet opportunity. In a moment of irresponsibility and passion, I became pregnant with our fourth child.

We had contemplated the idea of a fourth, liked the idea of a fourth, but were nowhere near ready to go down that road again. God apparently had a higher purpose and plan, because unbeknownst to us, sometime around that ignorant moment of bliss a beast from hell had been reawakened. If we had waited for our perfect timing, a fourth child would have been erased from the realm of possibility forever.

Jason interviewed for the job and did well, so well that he was called back for a second and a third interview—three separate interviews for one position. We were confident the job was his. However, before he departed, he was asked to complete one final requirement: filling out a health appraisal form. A few days later, we returned home to a disappointing email that informed us that they had filled the position with a "more qualified candidate." In other words, they didn't want to hire someone with a history of a brain tumor.

He found summer employment teaching tennis, both privately and in a club setting. This income provided a sense of financial relief, but in other aspects, April of 2009 was not enjoyable—for several reasons.

First, Lucas was screaming all day long, and nothing could or would soothe him. He was agitated, angry, and hurt, and we had absolutely no idea why. We went to the ear specialist, the emergency room, and his family doctor, but nobody had any answers for our little guy as he continued to bang his head with such intensity that his entire forehead bled at times.

Additionally, I was in the first trimester of pregnancy, a pregnancy we rejoiced and mourned simultaneously. We went into survival mode once again. I was nervous as my twenty-week ultrasound appointment approached during the first week of May. The ultrasound appointment with Lucas's pregnancy had been fiercely cruel, and I couldn't shake a feeling that I would hear the same dismal, heartbreaking report as I had five years prior. I was constantly cramping, undoubtedly stress related, which yielded some unique advice from my obstetrician—"Go home, take a bath, and have a glass of wine." He was aware of our situation and probably recognized that I needed to manage my stress in one way or another or the baby would be in jeopardy.

Finally, Jason's quarterly MRI was drawing near on June 15, and I was filled with nervous apprehension about that event. He seemed to be doing well, but he always seemed to be doing well. Jason did not show weakness. He would continue with life as usual until something literally knocked him out. Yes, he had a few symptoms, but we thought they were just the aftereffects of the past. We were fairly confident that the MRI would show no tumor regrowth.

Fast-forward to May. We brought Lucas to the neurologist and demanded an MRI. The test finally gave us an answer. He had Chairi Malformation, which meant his spinal cord was growing into his brain, causing intense headaches and pain. He also had a tethered spinal cord—a cord twisted tightly like a wet towel. A successful surgery to correct both problems was accomplished the first week of June.

Lucas recovered beautifully. He was confined to a full body splint for a week, where he would hold his "blankie'" and watch movies. Caleb would join him, trying to make Lucas smile as we monitored their bonding. The recovery was uneventful, and the head banging completely stopped.

At my twenty-week ultrasound the doctor assured me that the baby was progressing normally, and I exhaled that stress. The cramping also subsided as I began to relax; things were improving in our life.

Last, but not least, Jason's MRI. On a warm, summer morning, he left as usual to teach tennis and then excused himself around noon for his appointment. He checked in, signed the tedious paperwork, and laid his body flat on the table, subjecting his head to numerous rounds of radiation.

Thirty minutes later, the phone rang at home. I anxiously picked up the receiver and readied myself for the good news I anticipated. Instead, Jason's annoyance at the situation was clear.

"The tumor's back. I have to check myself into ER immediately."

CHAPTER 15

J Minus Jourteen Months

*"People brought all their sick to him and begged him to let
the sick just touch the edge of his cloak and all who touched
him were healed."*

Matthew 14:36

Oh God, I thought, *No, not again. Not after a year and a half of
clean reports. We finally have Lucas figured out. I'm having a
healthy baby, and we are back to square one with Jason? Please
God, let the tumor be benign again. God, I can't do this. Not with a six-
year-old, a handicapped four-year-old, a two-year-old, and an unborn
baby. Dear Jesus, have mercy!*

For the second time in two years, Jason was immediately admit-
ted for an early morning surgery while I began a frantic search for
babysitters. I was six months pregnant and extremely uncomfortable,
with the cramps reoccurring and my tiredness all-consuming.

In the hospital, Jason noticed my discomfort as I shifted from
side to side, trying to redistribute the weight into some form of relief,
and he graciously offered me his hospital bed. I laughed, "No! You
have a brain tumor!"

He insisted, and I climbed upon the bleach-drenched white sheets
and sank guiltily into some level of comfort. He sat in the chair and
joked with visitors about how his pregnant wife had it worse than he
did—he just had a brain tumor, no big deal.

His close friend scolded him, "Dude, it is a big deal. You have a brain tumor and four kids." Jason's typical reply, "It's not a big deal; I'll be fine."

The nurse said he could have two people beside him before his surgery. He replied, "I only need my wife."

But I didn't want to be brave anymore. I was exhausted from needing the emotional strength of a million people. I looked at my husband, ready to undergo a knife to his brain for the second time in two years, and thought, *Is this our life? Between Jason and Lucas, is this how the rest of my life will be? No rest? Like King David, fighting and weary all the time?*

Jason took my hand, and we prayed. Prayed for wisdom as skilled hands cut, prayed for a peace that passes understanding, and prayed for complete and total healing. As the nurses wheeled him away from my blurred vision, he smiled, "I'll be fine. I'm Superman remember?"

"Right," I whispered back, "but I've misplaced my Wonder Woman cape."

The surgery was successful. Once more the doctors removed all visible tumor, and now we were in familiar territory awaiting the biopsy results. I drove back and forth between home and the hospital, bringing the kids to see Daddy, leaving the kids behind with someone, anyone, who would take them so I could spend time with Jason. I felt constantly exhausted, as I had to will my body to continue moving despite the reality of an empty tank.

The moment we got the results of the biopsy, Jason was weary due to the medications and was lapsing in and out of consciousness. His mom, Holly, and I sat together, side by side, hands clasped in unity as the doctor arrived, a stoic look etched on his middle-aged face.

He hesitantly walked toward us, and as time stood still, said candidly, "The biopsy is back. It's a glioblastoma."

Brain cancer.

No, it can't be, was my first thought. I had done some research on tumors during the past year and a half. I was all too aware of what a glioblastoma diagnosis meant. Those who were served this news rarely lived to see two years. In fact, the average survival rate was exactly fourteen months. I nervously looked at the woman beside me, whose face had turned deathly pale upon hearing the news—the reality that her son had just been handed a death sentence.

"Okay, thank you," she whispered. She turned to me and said with a hint of braveness, "We will do what we have to do."

The doctor looked intently at both of us and muttered, "I am very sorry." With that, he left.

I slumped forward in the chair, head between my hands, unborn child between my legs, letting the words and their meaning sink into my soul. I wept. I wept for Jason, I wept for my children, and I wept because I didn't know how I was going to continue on.

I slept fitfully throughout the night, spending an hour or so in the waiting room and coming back periodically to check on mother and son. At 4 a.m. I was awakened by his mom. "Jess, Jason wants you. He's awake." He was confused about my whereabouts.

I stayed beside him throughout the night and into the next afternoon, finally leaving to tend to my abandoned children back home. As I turned to leave, I overheard my husband proudly bragging to the nursing staff, in a tremendously weak and hoarse voice, his plans to be discharged within forty-eight hours. They laughed and admonished him to "sit tight"; he still had to eat, walk, and have a bowel movement.

Those nurses were proven wrong exactly twenty-four hours later as Jason signed discharge papers and walked out of that hospital, tumor free for the second time. It was his signal to the world: he would not go down easily.

CHAPTER 16

Changing the Game

"Don't be afraid, just believe, and she will be healed."

Luke 8:50

The diagnosis of terminal cancer changed our game plan. The watch and wait option was no longer available; chemo and radiation were recommended as the only possible route, and we pursued it immediately. Jason started an intense round of treatments in August, handling the side effects well as he continued to work part-time subbing and personal training. He insisted on helping with the kids as much as possible, waking with Lucas each morning and caring for him before school, then resting in the afternoons and into the early evenings.

Baby Joshua arrived the following month, on September 15, 2009, with a scheduled C-section. The huge scar on the side of Jason's head attracted attention from most of the medical staff, who curiously inquired about it. He proudly declared that he had stage 4 brain cancer and insisted that he would be just fine; his God had healed him.

In the months leading up to Joshua's birth we had both come to an absolute, unshakeable faith that Jason would be healed here on earth. He had both an inner and an outer strength that I knew could withstand anything cancer or treatments would throw his way. The man I knew lived as a real-life superhero, and the way he had approached this battle so far had strengthened my faith both in our Lord and in my husband. Jason would not go down without giving it every single thing he had within him—this I knew beyond a shadow of a doubt.

As I recovered in the hospital from the C-section, Jason and I naïvely pitied the perceived lack of faith we saw in the doctors and nurses as they walked away with tears in their eyes, aware of the general outcome of this vicious disease and heartbroken for what the future held for our young family.

Joshua was a blessed distraction throughout the following year. Yes, having a newborn was difficult, but it took my mind off my harsh reality and reminded me of the continuous cycle of living and dying—both living in the physical and dying to ourselves daily as Scripture calls us to do (Galatians 2:20).

Jason did well with chemotherapy, and eventually the brain tumor drug Avastin was added to his regimen. This was an intravenous infusion that caused exhaustion for the patient receiving the cocktail. His chemo cycle consisted of one week on, three weeks off, with Avastin being administered biweekly.

On December 23, two days before Christmas, Jason was unexpectedly dismissed from his position at the holistic doctor's office. The official reason was "a lack of work"; the unofficial reason was likely tumor related. He struggled at home with an inability to concentrate, and it had probably trickled into his work environment. He was unemployed again except for the occasional substitute teaching position, which seemed to be more and more difficult to obtain. I was already weary with the demands of caring for a newborn baby, Lucas, a terminally ill husband, and two other children, plus teaching part-time. Now, again, I wondered where our income would come from.

One night, I stared at the stack of bills with no idea how we were going to pay them. I looked at Jason and asked, "Do you think you can apply for disability now?"

This had become a constant area of contention through the year—he did not want to admit that we needed help. He couldn't return my gaze, eyes full of shame as he softly replied, "Yes."

Making that decision, I believe, was one of the hardest things he ever had to do. His pride would not allow someone else to take care of his family, and he was not one to ask for handouts. Most people had no idea how desperate we were during those months. Laying down his pride was a completely selfless act, because in doing so, he was admitting that he could no longer take care of us. He only did it for his family, for me—to give me the gift of financial peace of mind in an otherwise tumultuous life.

I applied for disability the next day, and we were approved immediately. We began receiving $1,400 a month, absolutely life-changing money, along with food assistance. Fourteen hundred a month doesn't sound like much, but it paid the mortgage while his subbing and my teaching income paid the remainder of the bills. Jason could now rest when he needed to, and I could pay the bills when they arrived without searching our home for something to sell. Around the same time, he began a personal training job at a local YMCA. He worked only a few hours a week, but the opportunity gave him an emotional and physical outlet.

We drifted until March, when we received the news that the latest MRI showed an active tumor. This meant that the treatment protocol was no longer effective. We crossed our fingers and switched to a new chemotherapy, hoping the new treatment would eradicate the cancer once and for all—a very farfetched idea, but we remained optimistic, or at least I pretended to be optimistic. Honestly, I was so sick of it all, and instead of bringing it to God and allowing him to renew my spirit, I just ignored him for the most part—justifying the lack of relationship with the thoughts of *if he didn't make my life so insane, I would have time for him.* In other words, it was God's fault that I didn't lean on him.

Day in and day out, I was weary with the kids, and with Lucas in particular, who had his own special set of needs, and with a husband who was always tired. During this time, Lucas was screaming and head banging again, indicating a problem, and I prayed, which was rare during these hectic days, that his shunt was not to blame, nor anything bigger that would involve surgery.

I brought him to the neurologist on March 30, and the nurse determined that his shunt programming had failed. I thanked the Lord for an easy fix: just a twist of a knob on his shunt to readjust it, quick and painless, and he went back to being normal, happy Lucas.

Jason was a different story. His vision and memory seemed to be rapidly deteriorating as the cool, crisp spring air gave way to the longer, hotter days of summer. He was becoming increasingly disoriented and tired as we anxiously awaited the next MRI, scheduled for the beginning of May.

CHAPTER 17

He Gives and Takes Away

"Are you not much more valuable than they?"

Matthew 6:26

With this new journey underway, I began to write online updates for friends and family through Carepages.com.

May 6, 2010

Jason and I were watching our favorite show last night when we heard a very loud chirping coming from the deck. I looked at him with the knowing glance of "you go figure out what it is," because in the past it has meant that our "ferocious" cat has found a playmate. I know within the realm of nature it's eat or be eaten, but I don't want to see it taking place.

Jason got up to investigate the situation, and sure enough it was a little sparrow peeping away at the top of his lungs. He was just sitting there on our deck—hurt.

Soon Caleb comes walking into the room to see what's going on. After some deliberation, he decides to bring the bird to the slide on the top of his swing set to keep it safe for the night. (There's a point to this story, I promise, just keep reading . . .)

Nine-thirty rolls around, and Jason and I go to bed, and I can't get this dumb bird out of my head. I do devotions and pray desperately that God heal this bird. I kept thinking, *His eye is on the sparrow*, so how much more is his eye on my family?

Honestly, it was refreshing to beg God to heal something/someone other than Jason. Probably a coping mechanism on my part, but I'm believing and hoping that the bird is gone in the morning, because I can believe that it was healed and flew away (even if an animal got to it, I won't know and ignorance is bliss, right?).

Fast-forward to morning—I came downstairs and Jason said, "You just missed a Kodak moment." Apparently Caleb ran out this morning to check on his bird, and he came back with a sad look on face and said, "I think the bird is dead, but he might just be sleeping, but I'm pretty sure he's dead." I found myself tearing up over this thinking, "God, why didn't you just heal that dumb bird?"

Jason also had his oncologist appointment this morning, and his ride came to bring him. Our plan was that I would get the kids up and meet him down there. His doctor is always running late, and in theory if I made it down there at 9:00 a.m. I would probably make it just in time for the appointment. Of course this morning the doctor was on time, and I got a call at 8:45 from Jason saying that he's done already. I loaded the kids into the car and headed out to pick him up. I'm still thinking about the dead sparrow and just sad about it all when I turned on the car and the song playing on the radio is, "Take these broken wings and learn to fly again."

Aghhh, not what I'm in the mood to hear. Me learn to fly again if Jason dies? Jason learn to fly again after treatments? What, God??

I switch the channel to a Christian station, and "I'll Fly Away" is playing. What is going on with all of these bird songs? You have to understand, Josh's whole bedroom is devoted to the verse, "Are you not much more valuable than they?" With a big colorful tree and birds everywhere, it reminds me constantly how much we mean to God.

Enough of the radio; Mabel has been chattering constantly so I finally pay attention to what she's saying: "Mama, look, the birds are so beautiful!" This child does not mention birds on a daily basis. Again I'm thinking, What are you showing me God, what are you preparing me for, what is the deal with all of the birds?

Finally we arrived to where Jason was waiting to be picked up. He got into the car and turned to me. "The CAT scan showed that the tumor is growing; it's not responding to treatments, so we're going to look at other options including surgery." I sigh and think of all of the birds and how much God cares for them. He will care for my family.

We should have a plan in the next forty-eight hours. Our oncologist is discussing all of the options with Duke and Cleveland Medical Centers, which we have also consulted with. Pray for peace that passes understanding, overflowing wisdom for everyone involved, strength for the journey, and joy in every moment we have together.

Summer descended upon Michigan in full force, slamming into us with a hot stickiness as Jason began to rapidly deteriorate, his treatments becoming ineffective. He continued to rise every morning, feed and dress Lucas, and put him on the bus for summer school. I allowed him to accomplish these tasks until one morning when I awoke at 8:30 a.m. to find them both sitting on the front porch together, Lucas screaming in his wheelchair, his clothes on inside out. The bus had arrived an hour earlier, at 7:30.

This mishap officially ended a father-son tradition. It made me irate and incredibly heartbroken that such an insidious disease could steal every single thing from our lives: traditions, normalcy, a father, a husband. I was mad at Jason, mad at Lucas for being so difficult, mad at God, and mad at cancer.

I was now awake half the night with a baby and a terminally ill husband, and I got to roll out of bed at 7 a.m. to get Lucas on the bus, and he didn't even want me. He wanted his dad. He would scream—confused, murderous screams—because of the inexplicable change in his schedule.

The tragedy of brain cancer continued to manifest in many of our daily activities. I awoke very early one morning, around 2 a.m., to find Jason making pancakes. He was disoriented and half-blind, thinking morning had arrived, and in the process he almost burned the house down in the middle of the night. I found him in the midst of a cloud of smoke in the kitchen, trying to cook—trying to take care of us.

August 1, 2010

Jason has been on the new chemo treatment since Wednesday. I'm sure most of you can imagine the stress of our life right now, so I'll spare you the details, but overall, it is not easy. I keep thinking, if I can live through this, I can probably live through anything. He doesn't get out of bed anymore. I bring him all of his meals and meds and have to wake him just to have him swallow them. I'm trying to get his sugars under control because they may be contributing to some of the fatigue, but the reality is, he has stage four brain cancer, and he's been on poisons for over a year now, and he's beat. I don't see a lot of fight in him anymore, which is hard. I'm hoping that the Ritalin helps at some point. He was supposed to be in his sister's wedding over the weekend, but after observing him at the rehearsal, his sister and I realized that it just wasn't going to happen. He is very disoriented, confused, and tired. Pray for strength, peace, grace. It's hard to "just keep livin'" right now.

I continued to write updates online to let friends and family know how we were doing, but I certainly didn't share all of the gritty details, and the details, unquestionably, were not pleasant. Jason attempted his daily activities without assistance, prideful until the very end: getting out of bed, using the bathroom, making meals, falling down and becoming disoriented, lying in his food or worse yet, in his urine.

Everyone believed I was incredibly strong and faithful during these trials, but behind closed doors I struggled with anger, and my anger clouded the fact that my heart was breaking into a million pieces for my family, for the man I had married and vowed to love till death do us part. I could not comprehend why I couldn't have a normal life, why I wouldn't someday celebrate a fifty-year anniversary with my husband and our beautiful children.

I realize now that I used anger to express every other emotion I was feeling. Anger was safe. Anger clouded the pain, the anguish, the tears. Anger was something that could be directed at someone or something. Anger at my husband for having cancer. Anger at God for allowing me to become pregnant in 2004, in that specific moment. Why did that sperm make it? Did a defective sperm outrun all of the healthy sperm? Or was it a defective egg? Why couldn't God have prevented that sperm and that egg from ever meeting? Anger with my miraculous little boy, who was incredibly difficult while his father was ill. He didn't understand why his dad couldn't accomplish simple tasks for him anymore, why his father was confused and brought him the wrong sippy cup or put his diaper on backward. He didn't understand that his dad's brain was failing a little more every day as it was being ravaged by cancer.

Lucas would scream, banging his head against the floor in desperate agitation until blood dripped down his face. Later we found out he was having migraine headaches. I silently wished I had the courage to do the same: scream at the top of my lungs and hit something over and over again until my knuckles bled. I was angry that Jason and I had not acted like husband and wife for over a year because of the disease decimating his brain, taking every ounce of his life and leaving him with nothing to give outside of the pure determination to survive one more day. I was angry with myself because there was nothing I could do and nothing I could control to make the situation better. I had to obediently walk through the fires, and I felt like I was failing miserably.

I've learned that it is okay to question. It's okay to question life. It's okay to question God. Jason, filled with faith, struggled with questions as he fought to overcome brain cancer in May of 2010. Here is his Carepages entry from May 22:

> Is it too much to ask to be healed of cancer? Where the heck is the abundant life Jesus promised (John 10:10)? Not too long ago I was starting to feel like my old self again. Now I'm back to being useless. I stopped asking the "Why" and started asking God, "What now?" And you know what? IT'S NOT HELPING! I'm trying to be a good Christian throughout all of this but it's getting harder. Is it too much to ask to be done with cancer? At different points in my life I played professional tennis and owned my own fitness club. Now I can't even see straight to cut my lawn, let alone drive a freakin' car. My poor wife is stuck with so much to do, mainly because I'm useless. Is it too much to ask God to be healed? I've prayed so many times that something good would come of all of this and that God would be glorified. Is it too much to ask? There are days when I feel that this is it, and then I have days that I feel like I'm on a mountaintop with faith. I guess I should practice what I preach and not trust my feelings, but is it too much to ask to feel normal? I have moments where I just know everything will work out, and

I say to Satan, "Is that your best shot? Now let me show you mine!" I do believe all will work out for God's good purpose (Romans 8:28); I just don't always want to be nice about it. I want the abundant life Jesus promised. Is that too much to ask?

I constantly cleaned up after my husband, three-year-old Mabel, and Lucas, as well as catering to a baby's demands all day long. Thankfully Caleb was a very independent child and was more of a help than a hindrance.

I knew we were nearing the end, and that knowledge kept me going. I lived in a robotic fog, trying not to feel anything except anger toward the injustice of it all. I wailed at God in my quietest moments, no longer convinced that Jason would see an earthly healing but becoming resigned to what seemed to be the inevitable—he would receive a full healing when he entered heaven.

I say I was resigned—but at the same time, this knowledge didn't help me at all in my current reality. In fact, it also made me angry. God had healed Lucas—the weak one, the one who for all intents and purposes should have received his healing in heaven—but unless the miraculous occurred soon, it didn't look like an earthly healing was coming for Jason, the strong one, the one who could surpass all odds.

There was so much injustice in all of it. I loved my baby, my miracle boy, with everything within me, but he was difficult, and I needed his dad here to help me, and he couldn't help us in heaven! I screamed in desperation, the words caught in my throat. "God, why? You have taken everything from me, my family, my normal child, my children's father, my husband. What else can I give you?"

All I could do was come up and gasp for air, choking with each breath, tears streaming faster than I could wipe them away, feeling as if I were drowning in hell day after day.

I knew my days of living this way were numbered, that soon the quiet stillness of death would overtake the angry desperation.

My last shreds of belief in an earthly healing for Jason disappeared bit by bit as his body quickly deteriorated and his mind could no longer form many coherent thoughts. I struggled to understand God's will as he prepared my heart to accept Jason's death, and I mourned deeply for many lost opportunities in our marriage and family.

I also saw the struggle in Jason's eyes. He was growing weary of the fight. I knew that he struggled with leaving his earthly home, his wife, his four babies, but I saw in his eyes that he wanted to go, and that was hard on me too. It was as if God had given him a peace about his eternal healing but had forgotten to give me a peace about his leaving.

Jason's prayer was always that people would come to Christ through his hardships. Honestly, I didn't share this selfless sentiment. I didn't care if people were touched by our story in these moments, because I wanted my husband, and I wanted a normal, boring life as we raised our family together.

My tune slowly changed in the next few months as God continued to chip away at my perception of control. I began to accept that God was in control, and I was not. As I raged about everything he had taken from me, he would often remind me of his faithfulness, whether my ears wanted to hear it or not. *I have also given it all for you my child. I gave you my Son, my beloved Son, sent to die so that you might experience the darkness for only a time in comparison to the eternal reward I have planned for those who put their faith in me.*

I was determined to be strong for Jason's final days. I was exhausted by the end of each day, kids finally in bed, pouring myself glass after glass of wine, trying to settle my nerves, which were so incredibly raw during each hour throughout the day. It felt like a fairy tale gone extraordinarily wrong.

The Lord gives and the Lord takes away.

But at this point in the journey, I wondered if there was anything more he could take.

CHAPTER 18

Wheels on the Bus

"So that your faith might not rest on man's wisdom, but on God's power."

1 Corinthians 2:5

August 12, 2010 – Carepages entry

I knew from the moment I awoke this morning at 5:00 a.m. that this day was not going to top my list of favorite days. While getting Lucas on the bus we were singing the childhood song, "The wheels on the bus go round and round," and I started tearing up already at the thought of what the day held. Then while getting ready, I thought, no need for eye makeup, I'll probably just cry it off later this morning. Jason and I went to his oncologist appointment with Dr. Brinker, who took one look at Jason, all 159 pounds of him shivering in a wheelchair, and ordered an MRI for tomorrow. He will call me after the results to discuss our options. He also canceled Jason's Avastin treatment and told me to stop giving him his chemo pills—which indicates a lack of faith in the treatment protocol.

He looked at me with a knowing look, and my eyes started to tear up. "I know," I said, and he replied, "We'll discuss our options tomorrow."

Dr. Brinker is also ordering a hospital bed for our home to make it easier in terms of getting Jason up to eat, go the bathroom, etc. On the way home I heard one of my favorite songs by Francesca Battistelli—"Sunlight Burning at Midnight," "making my life something so beautiful, beautiful." I love that song but had never really thought about the words: "Like sunlight burning at midnight . . ."

It would be a miraculous thing to have the sun burning at the midnight hour, kind of like how my life probably looks right now; the miraculous would have to occur for it to look like something beautiful again. I feel like my world is going to bottom out in the next twenty-four hours, not that I don't have an idea of what's coming, but I just don't want to hear it.

It's also Lucas's sixth birthday today, my little miracle boy. God has blessed me so much through him and taught me so many life lessons. It's ironic that it's his birthday today with everything going on with Jason. When I got Lucas off the bus this afternoon he gave me a big smile and started singing, "The wheels on the bus go round and round." It was a huge boost to my heart, because he remembered that we were singing it this morning when I put him on the bus! He's never done that before. The Lord gives and the Lord takes away, blessed be the name of the Lord.

Some technical stuff that I've been meaning to post: Jason never checks his cell phone or his email anymore. If you want to get ahold of us, please call the house phone. Also, if you come to visit him, please don't talk about death or dying. He is not aware of how dire the circumstances are and still talks about opening his new gym. Tell him he looks great and he's doing well. Oh, and please call before coming over. We are great with having visitors, I'd just rather not be in my pajamas when you come. I have a feeling that the next few days could be emotionally tough; please let us digest everything for a day or two. Thank you for your love, support, prayers, and everything else.

My miracle boy's sixth birthday. We celebrated in one room while his father lay silent in another room, each of his breaths shorter than the previous one, his frail body rattled with defeat as he edged closer to eternity.

On August 13, the following day, I received a call from the oncologist saying that the tumor was stable. I could not comprehend this news. Jason had deteriorated so quickly in such a short amount of time that I didn't understand how the tumor could not be to blame. Two weeks prior he was still able to fake functioning as a normal person while hiding about 70 percent of his deficiencies. Now he looked really sick—dying sick, painfully thin, devoid of any muscle tone, with loose skin hanging off his bones. He was deathly pale and unable to stand or walk without assistance.

The news from the oncologist confused me. I had to make an extremely important decision about his treatments in the next twenty-four hours. My options included continuing the treatments, which seemed to be causing his deterioration, stop the treatments and hope that the tumor remained stable, or try an alternate plan.

The news made me want to continue the treatments, but my heart was telling me differently. I, along with hundreds of prayer warriors—friends, family, and those unknown who had read about my story as it circulated far and wide via Carepages, the local news, and other social media sites, prayed throughout the night for direction and wisdom regarding what route I was to take.

* * *

In the last few weeks, Jason had begun accepting the reality of his limitations, as it became increasingly difficult for him to muster up the energy to train his one or two clients a week—yes, he was still training clients even though he could hardly move the other twenty-two hours in a day. One evening, his supervisor from the YMCA called. She informed me through tears that they would be terminating his employment. The night before he had wandered aimlessly around the club, unable to see or comprehend where he was or why he was there, stumbling and falling over exercise equipment as people looked on in despair and sorrow.

After the news of his termination, Jason no longer rose from his bed, and he began to see glimpses of the other side. Heaven was far superior to what our broken world could offer him. Often, in his weakness, he would relate what he was seeing beyond, and in the same short breaths, he would offer me reassurance that the next world was not to be feared; instead, it was simply a rebirth. I began to think through this idea of death being a rebirth by using my recent pregnancy experiences as tools to gain a better understanding of what he was trying to explain. My four children, prior to birth, had only known my womb until the day they unexpectedly burst forth into a new life and fell into my loving arms, their mother. I started to view death in a similar way. We all live in Earth's womb, which is all we know, and through the painful contractions of death, we are thrust down the birth canal into a magnificent new existence, falling into the waiting arms of our heavenly Father. It was easier for me to accept Jason's departure as I viewed it this way.

I began to accept that our time together as a family was becoming increasingly limited, and in the process, I started a frantic crusade of making memories for the kids. I took pictures every chance I had, which in turn made Jason upset—"Stop doing that, I am not going to die."

I also wanted him to write letters to the kids, but I knew I was not the one to conduct such an emotional task with him. I was trying hard to compartmentalize my emotions, shoving the pain deeply away so that I could function as his caretaker and the mother of our children. I prayed about who the right person was for this sensitive and emotional responsibility. I kept hearing the name Paula.

Paula was a fellow trainer at the YMCA, and she would often volunteer to bring Jason to his appointments. I didn't know her well other than through her relationship with Jason as a chauffeur and fellow employee. It felt strange to ask her to assist in this task, but I did so anyway, hesitantly saying, "I've been praying about this idea, and I keep hearing your name."

After I explained, she replied, with eyes full of tears, "It would be an honor. My dad died when I was five, and my stepdad died a few years after. I always wondered what they would have said to me if given the chance."

She came a few times a week, sitting with Jason, talking to him, and often he would say to her, "I'm so confused. Am I hanging on for a life here, or am I preparing to die?" She comforted him with the knowledge that only God knew.

Paula would not shed a single tear as a dying man relayed his final thoughts to his children. She wrote verbatim what his heart poured out and then walked out two glass doors, closed the curtain, and sobbed. He never saw her tears; she remained strong for him and steadfast in telling him that he was "looking good," even going so far as to help him work out in bed while in fact his "outward man was wasting away, yet inwardly [he was] being renewed day by day" (2 Corinthians 4:16).

In return, she received an idea of how her dads had felt toward her, even though they had never been able to leave her a letter.

At the end of her sessions with him, when he was no longer able to verbalize a coherent thought, she handed me the precious notebook. I gingerly fingered the stark, white notebook pages, hesitantly glancing at the words they held as the tears dripped from the corners of my eyes once again. I reached for her hand, squeezed it tightly, and thanked her for the gift she had given me and my children.

Later that night I tucked the notebook away in our safe. I wasn't in a mental or emotional place where I could actually read and dwell on the words, and only Caleb would be capable of even understanding them at this point. Soon enough, I would revisit the notebook, linger over its contents, and let the tears flow, but for the time being, the pages would be held safely within the confines of lock and key— pages holding priceless messages of encouragement from Jason that the children would treasure one day.

Dear Caleb,
I'm so proud of you for how you've been handling everything with my cancer and with Lucas. I thank God every day for how smart you are, and I can't wait to see what you become. Keep being a big help to Mom. Someday when we meet in heaven, you can teach me all the things you learned while I was gone. Go ahead and try to catch one more big fish for us.

Love you,
Dad

Dear Mabel,
I love you. I can't wait to see you walk down the wedding aisle. I will be there to see how beautiful you are. You are my little princess, and I can't wait to see you as a queen.

Love, Dad

Dear Lucas,
I'm so proud of how far you've come. Nobody can believe how well you are doing. In the last year you went from not being able to walk to walking! I love that I get to brag about you every day. I'll walk with you someday. I love you.

Dad

Dear Josh,
I love having another son in my life. You, Caleb, and Lucas have made it so much fun for me. Don't forget to take care of your sister. Keep getting bigger and stronger every day. I love you with all my heart, and these swords will be ready for you and Caleb in a few years.

Love, Dad

CHAPTER 19

Ultimate Healing

"Blessed is the man who perseveres under trial, because when he has stood the test, he will receive the crown of life that God has promised to those who love him."

James 1:12

August 14, 2010

Today was a tough one emotionally. I wrestled all night with the decision, replaying all of the conversations Jason and I had had before it got bad: "I'd rather die on the operating table than get to a point of uselessness"; "I want to go out swinging"; "I never want my kids to see me need help to the bathroom." By morning I had decided to keep him on the treatments. Then the next few hours played out in ways that I will not go into for the sake of his pride. I thought, *There comes a time when a person with brain cancer cannot make these decisions anymore and someone else needs to make them in his place.* I could not bring him his chemo pills today. We are done with treatments for now.

Those nights, each ending a nightmarish day, I bathed in quiet stillness. The house was calm, the kids and Jason asleep, and I slowly sank all the way under the water and lay there imagining that death might feel similar. Seconds later, I gradually rose to the surface with the light of the moon coming through the window to welcome and embrace my surfacing.

I imagined the entrance into heaven feeling somewhat like this, with the emergence of the naked soul rising from the watery, eternal realm and into the light of the Sovereign God. That is what I imagined, trying as hard as humanly possible to understand the hereafter my husband was about to experience.

In a sense, I was jealous. Jealous of him experiencing something so out of my realm of comprehension, jealous of the glory he was about to behold, and jealous that he was about to checkout from the pain of it all. He would not have to raise four children alone and go through life being a complete pity case. He would not have to hear for the one millionth time, "How are you?" and answer with hot tears in check. And he would not have to eat casserole after casserole after casserole because he didn't have the energy to even cook for those four kids he was left with.

Jason was about to rise above the tide into a light I could only imagine, something so beautiful, so completely astounding, something that I imagined would contain more beauty than even sunlight burning at midnight.

August 14, 2010

I have three meetings in the next twenty-four hours with hospice care. When people ask what they can do, I say pray. Pray that I make the right decision on who will be involved with Jason's care. Pray that I can keep my head above water. Pray for strength beyond normal human strength, and as always, peace that passes understanding. "My life, something so beautiful, beautiful" . . . right?

And so the decision was made, right or wrong or somewhere in between. There was no turning back now. I had arrived upon the doorstep of hospice, the point of no return. The point of no more hope, no more questions about cancer, and no more answers either.

All of my questions and answers would now be about *when.* When would it be over? When would death overcome his body? When would he leave us?

And how the hell was I supposed to choose which organization would help my husband die? It was all so surreal.

I have the utmost respect for hospice, but it's still hard to accept the reality that you are choosing an organization to walk you through *the valley of the shadow of death* with your loved one. And my loved one was a thirty-three-year-old man, a young man, the father of my four children. *How in the world did he end up here? How did I end up here?*

August 16, 2010

The hospice decision has been made, and I have a peace about the organization that I've chosen. I never knew there were so many steps to the death process. I think that's our society. We try to make everything neat and tidy, in its proper place, but there's nothing neat and tidy about death. It is probably the biggest nightmare I will ever walk through. It's helpful that they come in and take care of his basic needs, but I feel like I have totally lost control of my life. There is no normal anymore. According to the death manual that they gave me (yes, there is a manual for dying), we are probably in the final week or two. As I read it, I literally fell to the floor crying, with Mabel saying, "It's okay, Mama. It's okay." It's one thing to know in your heart that the end is near, but to actually read the facts, in black and white, is something else. His nurse agrees that it probably won't be long.

I try to be honest in these entries, and part of me felt some relief in hearing those words. There is very little life left in him. He is definitely distancing himself from this life. He has no desire to watch television, read, or listen to music. I am in a complete robotic fog right now, but I know that when the dust settles, there will be more than enough time for the reality to hit me. Now I want to honor him and our marriage by pulling it together and getting through this with the kids. I have been mourning for a long time. I've gone through so many stages of grief already with the knowledge that I probably won't see a fiftieth or even a fifteenth wedding anniversary with this man who is my best friend. I'm so sick of being so naked to the whole world. Most people when asked how they're doing can pull off a fine, good, or okay. I can't. I am in no way fine, good, or okay. My husband is dying and leaving four children. There is nothing okay about it.

Someone said to me recently, "You were always so confident in your belief that Jason would be healed." I still am—I am 100 percent confident that he will be healed. I don't put God in a box, and he will heal Jason either here or in heaven. My faith is supposed to help me through this, and it does. I know Jason will be healed completely, and I try to know that God has a plan for my life, but I don't understand it at all. I think, how can the plan be me raising these kids alone or another guy raising these kids that aren't his? How can the perfect plan not be Jason staying here with us and raising his own kids? I guess that's the faith aspect of it all, but it doesn't make the pain any easier to bear.

For some of my children, Jason's illness was simply a part of their life. Mabel and Joshua had never known him not sick. Mabel's earliest memories of her father involved his shaved head and how he loved to toss her on his lap as she giggled with delight. As Jason progressively became worse, his strength diminishing daily, he would lie in bed more frequently, and she began to struggle with bouts of sadness and confusion. She would sit on the sofa for hours on end, watching cartoons while sucking her thumb and holding her special blanket. She instinctively knew that something was wrong in her world, and I felt her sadness as my own.

In an attempt to have some one-on-one time with her and also, in the process, forget reality for a few hours, I brought her to the park, a one-time special day for just the two of us, and we played together in childish innocence for hours. When we left, we were refreshed and renewed, ready to tackle the remaining days we had to be a family, which felt like it was falling apart a little more day by day.

Lucas was bored, not understanding where his playmate had gone, and I had no way to explain to him that his daddy was lying in bed, struggling with every ounce of his strength to remain with us for as long as possible, and that he had no stamina left to play with any of his four young children.

Caleb, as always, was my right-hand man. He took over where Jason failed as he assumed a leadership role that far surpassed his young six years. He helped me immensely during that period in ways that he will probably never understand. I leaned heavily on him and he back on me; I withheld very few truths from him in regard to the severity of his father's condition, and in return, he trusted me and obeyed instantly when I needed his assistance with chores, his father, his handicapped brother, or even just holding baby Joshua yet again as I rushed around trying to accomplish way too many tasks for one woman to handle.

All I really remember about those final days is a whole lot of crap—literally. We had four family members in diapers, Lucas and Joshua with horrible diarrhea. Each morning as I retrieved Lucas from bed, I was greeted with the stench of something putrid. He would be covered in poop, head to toe, his bedding filthy and the walls around his bed smeared with the smelly excrement. And I would just weep. That bed felt like a metaphor for my life. My husband remained intensely stubborn and adamantly believed he could make it to the bathroom unassisted. Without fail, he would rise in the middle of the night, trying to make his way to the bathroom, and every night I would awaken from a light sleep to the sound of him falling on the floor and emptying his bladder wherever he happened to land, because in his cancer-ridden brain he believed he had made it to the toilet.

My mornings consisted of changing numerous diapers, cleaning Lucas's bedding, sometimes cleaning Josh's bedding, scrubbing Lucas and Josh down from head to toe, cleaning Jason's bedding and carpet, and wiping my husband down to the best of my ability until the hospice nurse came to do his official grooming. I hope that doesn't come across as disrespectful, but it is the reality of brain cancer. Brain cancer steals a person's abilities, their drive, their skills, their ambition, their mind, and in the end, their pride.

* * *

The first week into hospice care went well other than having people in and out of my house all day—nurses caring for Jason, feeding him, bathing him, and brushing his teeth. He would still talk to me and the kids and whoever came to visit, although he was disoriented and most of what he said did not make sense. Occasionally a glimmer of the old Jason would resurface, and for a brief moment I would have renewed hope that maybe, just maybe God was going to heal him here on earth . . . but the moment would pass quickly when the evidence of how much brain cancer had destroyed already would exhibit itself in one of the numerous physical, mental, or emotional manifestations in Jason's body.

Looking back, all of the literal crap in my life seems symbolic of how I felt about my life at the time—it was crap heaped upon crap. As much as I believed, or had faith, or knew a peace that passes understanding, the reality was that there were still hardships, pain, and tears to wade through. Christ's own words were, "In this world you will have trouble. But take heart! I have overcome the world" (John 16:33).

It was this promise I learned to hold to desperately, a promise I will not even necessarily understand in this lifetime, a promise that Christ did indeed overcome the world. The here and now will not last forever. Christ overcame the here and now. He overcame cancer, tears, pain, and everything else our sinful world throws at us.

And in that promise is the expectation of something worth enduring for: he took our crap so we might take on his promise of eternal glory.

CHAPTER 20

Good-byes

"It is written, 'No eye has seen, no ear has heard, no mind has conceived what God has prepared for those who love him.'"

1 Corinthians 2:9

August 22, 2010, was the night I lost Jason.

The night began with my routine. I put the kids to bed around eight and joined Jason in the den where he slept. I wasted time on the computer, probably Facebook—anything completely mindless and devoid of thought. Facebook had become my social life, my link to humanity in a world where I no longer felt comfortable, although in many ways I had become more connected to the body of humanity through pain, suffering, and the heartaches we all endure.

On this particular evening, I relished the stoic, emotionless silence as my husband lay across the room, unmoving, breathing deeply and methodically in and out. Around eleven I decided to lie down beside him on the mattress we had set up.

Approximately one hour later I awoke to an intense moaning sound.

Jason had never complained of pain—not once. He had pain throughout his treatments, but he never complained about it. This night was different. He sounded severely wounded, tortured in an incomprehensible way, devoid of all hope. He groaned with such a depth of pain, with an out-of-this-world anguish, as if all three years of fighting had finally caught up with his body and found him completely depleted of strength.

His groans became intense demands for relief. I was afraid and confused because I was giving him the same dosages of pain medication he had been taking for the past week, and nothing was touching this new level of agony. He sat upright, rocking back and forth, grabbing his head and screaming to the heavens for relief. With each minute of agony, he seemed to take a few steps closer to earning his crown of glory. While I sat helplessly by, he spoke to angels, asking them to carry him into heaven, and he spoke to a friend who had died years earlier of brain cancer. He reflected on his life, his children, and asked me, "How will I remember the kids?" And then he answered in the next breath, "Their hands will just be bigger."

As he inched closer and closer to his eternal destiny, God comforted him with a snapshot of my future. He turned and asked me, "Where is your husband?"

My mind flashed back to the horribly rude doctor who had spoken those same words on that terrible day when Lucas was diagnosed in utero.

I answered, "Honey, you are my husband."

He replied, "No, I'm not. When did you have six kids?"

Confused, I answered "I don't have six kids. We have four children."

He answered firmly, "No, you have six kids."

As the night slowly forged on, his pain grew unbearably intense.

Abruptly he declared, "Today is the last day I am going to be in this bed."

With my eyes full of tears I asked, "Why? Are you going home?"

He replied softly, "Yes. Tell your story."

His last words were a reference to a favorite movie of ours, *Moulin Rouge*. In one scene, the dying heroine, Satine, admonishes her young lover to "tell a story." Jason had encouraged me throughout our marriage to "tell my story." He always believed in my ability to keep it real through my writing, and he also knew that I had a deep desire to be a writer. It was his belief that God had chosen me to go through these trials as a badge of honor—God saw me as a vessel who could handle the fight, not unlike himself, and as someone who would tell her story to encourage others who had lost all hope.

Those were the last words I heard from him. With tears spilling down my face, I called hospice because I could not make him comfortable, regardless of my numerous attempts to do so. The nurse on call told me to open the box containing the lethal dosages of morphine that had been reserved for this occasion. "Give him the maximum dosage," she said.

I did. Immediately the moaning and groaning, the screams, the grabbing of his head, it all stopped, and he slipped into a medically induced coma. He no longer spoke. He no longer looked at me, or reached for me, or even seemed to recognize his surroundings. He had entered a new dimension where he would patiently wait until the angels were summoned to carry him home.

August 22, 2010, was the night Jason left life as we know it. Although he was still present in a physical body, that was the night I lost my husband.

CHAPTER 21

Praising in the Storm

"Be faithful, even to the point of death."

Revelation 2:10

"You can be as mad as a mad dog at the way things went.
You could swear, curse the fates, but when it comes to the
end, you have to let go."

from the movie *The Curious Case of Benjamin Button*

August 23, 2010. We waited, that long, drawn-out day, a day that felt like it would never end. People in and out, greetings—maintaining an emotionless, tearless, blank face—and then returning to Jason's room to lie down beside him.

A dear friend who had lost her husband to brain cancer a year earlier had given me valuable advice: "When it comes to the end, drop everything, even your kids, and lie down beside him until it is over." I heeded this instruction, leaving only to eat, nurse the baby, and put the kids to bed.

Jason had said he was only going to be in that bed for one more day, so I knew the end was near. He would not be completely accurate in his prediction . . . but he was eerily close.

There were frequent visitors in and out of our house: friends, family, people coming and going, all wondering, watching, and waiting. It is a surreal experience to wait for death. Waiting to give birth or waiting for a new job or a vacation I knew how to do, but I wasn't sure how to appropriately wait for my husband to die. As I waited, I made a list of his favorite songs to be sung at the funeral. I had picked out a cemetery plot, and now all there was left to do was wait.

I lay beside him, talking about our life together, talking about how I would make him proud, promising that I would tell our story, praying for him, quoting Scripture, telling him about the visitors who came, but he never responded. He just lay there and waited patiently and quietly for the perfect, graceful, and merciful moment to arrive.

A night passed, and Jason was still with us. The waiting continued. I again lay beside him throughout the day, leaving only when absolutely necessary to eat or nurse baby Joshua. The sky darkened as another day ended. The three youngest kids had been put to bed, but Caleb was still awake, talking with the two people left at the house—two of his aunts, my sister and sister-in-law. Everyone reasoned that Jason could hold on for another week or two or three; he was Jason, after all. If anyone could outlast a prediction it would be him.

The house was quiet, so I decided to put Caleb to bed, not having spent much time with him over the previous days. I leaned over and whispered to Jason, "I'll be right back. I'm putting Caleb to bed."

The next five minutes would be the only moments Jason had been left alone in days. Whenever I left, I would find a backup watcher—his mom, brother, sister, or dad, someone to keep the vigil going, anyone to ensure he would not be alone.

I went to retrieve Caleb and asked if he wanted to say good night to his father. He agreed—something Jason, in the precise calculations he had made in whatever dimension he was in, had not planned on. His son entered the subdued room, glanced quietly down at his father, and said, "Mom, he's dead."

He silently walked away.

Moments define our lives. Moments of grace and moments that feel like the absence of grace. Moments of complete loneliness and moments of knowing we never truly walk alone.

Jason took those precious moments alone to walk into eternity, hand in hand with his Savior. And it was in those moments that I felt what it truly feels like to experience complete and utter loneliness.

"What?" I gasped, glancing down upon the frail body of my husband and searching deeply into his absent eyes.

"What?!" My voice rose with emotion as I grabbed his warm shoulders and shook them violently with no response.

"How?" I screamed, gasping as tears streamed down my face, so many thoughts running through my mind. "How could you die in the five minutes I left you alone?!" I knew he had never expected Caleb to find him. I'm sure he thought, *She'll put Caleb to bed and come back to find me gone.*

"Dammit!" I screamed at God, at Jason, for me, my life, the immense pain and unfairness of it all. I fell to my knees, blubbering as the wetness ran freely all over my face, feeling the saltiness against my lips which were slightly agape, slightly parched and completely speechless over what had just occurred. I tucked my head between my knees, swaying back and forth, moaning—a deep lament for the sacred, horrific moment I had just witnessed. I mourned my dead thirty-three-year old husband and mourned myself, a thirty-three-year old widow with four small children.

I leaned over the silent body, his short, harsh breaths finally silenced, frantically feeling up and down his cool flesh with my hands—searching for a sign of life, searching for the lie within it all, and only feeling the coldness of death in return. His death. Jason's death. The death of our marriage, our vows fulfilled as I felt a presence ripping off of me. I will never be able to fully explain that feeling, but his immediate absence felt similar to the worst punch in the stomach imaginable—like someone knocking every bit of air out of my lungs and leaving me completely breathless. Jason was no longer physically a part of me, our marriage, or our family.

He stared blankly into the night, his body depleted of life, his soul on a journey to his eternal home. It was finished. The sheer, transparent despair and loneliness fell on me like a weighted fog, a smoky, dense, can't-catch-your-breath kind of haze.

I wept. I wept for my best friend, wept for our family, wept for my children, and wept because the journey was finally over.

In true Jason style, he'd had the final word, even in death. I gave him one moment, and he seized it, letting go on his own terms, alone, and valiantly without the help of anyone.

I know beyond a shadow of a doubt that he faced death squarely in the face and said, "Is that your best shot? Now let me show you mine!"

And I know, with his Savior cheering him on, that he thoroughly delighted in sending fear and death back to their eternal damnation in the fiery pit. I'm pretty sure he and Christ shared some high fives over that defeat as he entered those pearly gates.

August 24, 2010

Jason Thomas Crisman received his final treatment last night at 9:00 p.m. when he was escorted into the arms of the Ultimate Healer. Praise God, this treatment wiped the cancer out of his body completely. He is now healed and whole. I told him, I'll see you soon . . . but not too soon. I'm so happy he's not in pain anymore, yet so lonely at the reality that I've lost my best friend, my husband, and the father of my children.

"The Lord gives and the Lord takes away. Blessed be the name of the Lord."

In her book *The Healer*, author Dee Henderson wrote of death, "It feels very alone. Death is like a cloud coming near that shadows and blocks the color from life." But I don't believe that death feels very alone for the one dying. As I watched Jason during his final days, I saw a man struggling with leaving the mundane life he knew for a glimpse of the beauty he saw beyond the veil. His struggle was not in leaving this world, our sinful earth; instead, his struggle was in leaving his family. He was not one to leave those he loved stranded. Jason loved the movies *Braveheart* and *Gladiator.* He exemplified those characteristics of faithfulness and duty as a husband and father.

There was one more letter that Jason had written in those memorable sessions with Paula. A letter full of grace and thankfulness in spite of the anger and confusion he had experienced and witnessed so often during those difficult days. A letter full of hope. A letter for me.

August 10, 2010

Dear Jessica,

Thank you so much for taking care of me. I don't know where today is or where you are reading this, but I love you and can't wait to see you again. We fulfilled all our wedding vows in ten years. The greatest thing you will ever learn is just to be loved and love in return (Moulin Rouge). Come What May.

Love

Me.

In the end, I believe Jason was given a glimpse of my life without him, and he saw that I would be taken care of. I would have a blessed life beyond the immediate sorrow of his death. I believe he listened to his Savior's voice and obeyed the call to enter into his eternal reward where he heard the words, "Well done good and faithful servant."

One journey had ended. I exhaled, deeply and purposefully, for the first time in years. I exhaled despair, anger, and franticness and inhaled a confused blankness, a stillness, a quiet I had not felt in a long time.

And along with the newfound reprieve arrived an intense feeling of loneliness that in many ways felt like a deeper hell than the one I had just walked through.

CHAPTER 22

Inappropriate Widow

"We live by faith, not by sight."

2 Corinthians 5:7

Jason's funeral was held on a tennis court on the hottest day imaginable. A day earlier I went shopping to find an appropriate outfit for a thirty-three-year-old widow to wear. I walked around the mall dazed, trying to take in the reality of what I was purchasing. None of these events seemed real. They were more like a thick fog I was struggling to make my way through, a fog I would eventually awaken from and realize that everything had been a really horrible dream. I chose a black lace shirt and a black skirt that hung on my frame, which was painfully thin due to the endless weeks of stress and lack of nourishment.

I awoke the following morning, the day of the funeral ceremony, after a fitful attempt at sleep helped along by merlot and sleeping pills. I dressed the kids, curled my hair, put on makeup, and spent a few moments writing a good-bye letter that would be placed in Jason's coffin.

I stumbled onto the tennis court in uncomfortable high-heeled shoes, not something I was accustomed to wearing on a regular basis. I felt as if they represented my current emotional state, stumbling and uncomfortable in my new life.

I took a seat in one of the cheap fold-up chairs as droves of people began swarming in upon the hot asphalt courts to say their final good-byes. A large family picture, the last photo we had taken only weeks earlier, was lovingly placed at the front of the service.

I sat still and silent beside Caleb, who was dressed in black pants, a light blue shirt, and a tie, all of seven years old, with new weight on his shoulders as the man of the family and the old weight removed, as he no longer had to bear the responsibility of helping to care for his dying father. He was weary and relieved, just like his mother was.

We sat there, the two of us, sweat dripping down our expressionless faces, mine hidden behind thick, black sunglasses, his staring unwaveringly ahead, unflinching at the pain in front of him. Here we all sat, mourners in our black attire, the men dressed in suits, sweating profusely, but not one complaint escaping any of our lips. So entirely fitting to honor a man who loved nothing better than to break a good sweat on the tennis court and have others break a good one in the gym.

Jason was laid to rest at the cemetery near our home, where we would frequently walk as a family. In the past, he and I had jokingly picked out our grave sites, and I put him as close as possible to the one he had picked out.

As the casket lowered into the ground, the bagpipes belted out his favorite song, "Amazing Grace," and his children threw yellow roses into the crevices surrounding his final resting place—roses which symbolized his eternal dwelling spot, heaven. I buried my letter with him, a letter promising him that I would continue to live and that everything we had been through together would be used for God's glory. It was all very poetic: the young father; his children left behind, not really understanding the significance of the day or how it would change their lives forever; and the widow, dressed in black, stoic-faced and determined to put one foot in front of the other.

But poetry is not very comforting in the end.

The celebration of life ceremony was held immediately after the burial, a ceremony filled with love, tears, and joy. I looked in awe at the people who had come out to show their love and support for me and the kids. People spoke, one after another, telling stories of joy and remembrance of how this young man had touched their lives in one way or another, but I had no words in those moments. I felt alone and abandoned, not trusting myself to say anything, so I let those around me do the talking.

After the celebration ceremony, many of Jason's friends and family met up at a bar, not really knowing how else to appropriately honor a man they had called friend for so many years. In many aspects, this seemed like the perfect way to end an emotional three-year ride, but when they invited this newly widowed mom to tag along, I found myself declining.

I was exhausted. I needed rest. Rest from it all: the three years of battle, death, planning the funeral, the torment in my mind. Lots of rest. And I needed to get alone with God, because he had some explaining to do.

People pleaded with me, asking me to please allow someone to come home with me, to comfort me and stay with me, but I declined their well-meaning suggestions. I needed to face grief on my own terms. It would be entirely too easy to hide behind people and the busyness of good-hearted friends and family.

I was numb and emotionless on that long car ride home with four restless children, and as I pulled up to the last stoplight, I looked down at the ring upon my hand—a beautiful diamond etched with the words "Till death do us part." Something in me snapped, and I knew the ring on my finger represented a lie. I was no longer a married woman. I no longer had a husband, and the ring embodied a potential disenchantment with reality which I was in no way willing to entertain. I immediately ripped the silver band off, put it in my purse, and never put it back on again. I have never once regretted that decision.

Jason and I had our "till death do us part" moment. When he died, I literally felt something depart from me. The Bible talks about how the two shall become one, and when I felt the sensation of him leaving, I knew without a doubt that we were no longer one in a marital sense; Jason was gone, my marriage was done, and this was my new life.

I accepted my plight in that moment. I accepted it all. It was also there that I vowed, no matter what, to put one foot in front of the other and live for my kids and for a very distant belief that God still had a plan for my life.

My children were not going to lose two parents in 2010. By the grace and mercy of God Almighty himself, their mother was going to pick herself up and fake it until she made it.

September 10, 2010

It has been two weeks since I officially became a widow. This isn't a term that seems to fit me very well. I fit into the single mother category or just plain single but widow feels so old and worn—not an appropriate title for a thirty-three-year-old. People ask me how I'm doing and I answer "fine" (I was married to Jason for ten years and have his answer down pat), and then they ask, but how are you really doing? Again, the answer is fine. Not great, not horrible, just fine.

The day Jason died, cancer died as well. Brain cancer is a cruel, cruel taskmaster, and to have her off my back is somewhat of a relief. Watching Jason go through the dying process all summer long was the worst pain I will probably ever experience. Seeing him reduced to shreds—fighting to see, hear, eat, drink, talk, and finally breathe—was far worse than when it was finally over and he was healed.

The reality that my husband could die as a young man hit me the day we heard the words "brain tumor" three years ago. Since then I've been able to process and grieve through this idea, which has helped tremendously for the here and now. I've been in a storm since May, which is about the time that Jason really started struggling. It has been a raging, whipping storm, and then the storm was finally over and it was still overcast, cloudy, and gray, but—there is a calm, a peacefulness now that I haven't felt in a while. After every storm there is a cloudy overcast, but when it clears the sun always shines. I have faith that we will see the sun. Even with four kids, I can breathe again. It literally felt like as Jason was taking his last breath, I finally exhaled.

In hindsight, looking back through the years, I see hints of God preparing me for this journey, and in that preparation has been an immeasurable amount of grace and peace that I can't explain. The big wake-up call came early this summer with the death of the sparrow. The day that happened I wrestled all night with what I felt in my heart. I rebuked the devil, I screamed at God, but I knew what the sparrow was about, and I hated it. When there was still hope that God would heal him, I cried and cried and begged God to intervene, like David and Bathsheba with their infant son, but when God said no to my version of healing, I got up and said, "Thy will be done."

David's explanation parallels my thoughts in many ways: "While the child was still alive, I fasted and wept. I thought, who knows? The Lord may be gracious to me and let the child live. But now that he is dead, why should I fast? Can I bring him back again? I will go to him but he will not return to me" 2 Samuel 12:22. That's how I feel. When he died all that was left was his shell, and it wasn't him. I have a lot of life to live yet, God willing.

Jason and I had a fairy-tale life. No, it wasn't always perfect, but all in all we had a great marriage. He was a wonderful, faithful husband and father. His end was so Jason-like. He loved the movie *Braveheart* and anything representing laying down your life for another. Through his death many people reevaluated their own lives, priorities, and relationship with God. Jason would have it no other way: it was his race to run, and he ran it with faithfulness.

Now I have my race to run without him, but God has a plan. Some days it seems like a very distant plan, but I know he has a plan. The hardest part is the fact that I will never be married to Jason again. I know I'll see him soon but not too soon . . . but he will never again be my husband or a father to his children. I guess it's a faith thing, that what heaven has to offer must be so far superior to what I know here on earth, and when I get there, it won't matter anymore.

I've learned a lot on this journey about God's heart for his children, about my ideas of faith, healing, speak it and believe it, and so on. I will say one thing, none of us has it all figured out. It's easy to think we do when things are good, but God is not a formula. If he was, the control would be in our hands, and it's not. I've also learned that whether or not someone goes home or has their healing here on earth has nothing to do with the amount of faith they have. Jason had the faith to move the mountain, Lucas is evidence of that, but sometimes God says no to our plans and all we can say is, "Blessed be the name of the Lord." Sometimes having faith involves something much bigger and better than the here and now.

So again, we're fine. We're not great, but we're okay. There is this big void in everything I do throughout the day. A void in the number of dishes I wash (he ate a lot!), a void in the laundry, a void in the fact that the second sink in our master bathroom never has to been cleaned anymore because it's never used, and on and on. With the void is an easiness that I'm not sure what to do with at this point. I think I'll probably have to work through this in the coming months, because I have more time than I've had in a while.

My biggest struggle is loneliness, and there is nothing to do to fix it. I just need to walk through it. There is no checklist to work through, no steps to take, just time and relying on God's peace. Caleb is doing remarkably well; he was the one I was most worried about. He talks about Jason and what he's probably doing in heaven and how he misses him but he knows he's healed. Mabel is sad; she doesn't understand where Daddy went and looks for him every morning. There is some comfort in the fact that she won't remember in a year or two, but if a three-year-old can be depressed, I think she might be. Pray her through. Lucas and Josh are fine; they really weren't impacted a whole lot from what I can tell.

I'm done working and just enjoying being a mom, getting back to living, taking an online class, and thinking I might volunteer at the hospice organization that worked with Jason. I promised him the day he died that these kids wouldn't lose one parent to cancer and the other to depressive grief, so no, I'm not curled up in a corner overcome with grief. I'm living and enjoying these four little blessings that remind me so much of their father.

"Don't cry because it's over, smile because it happened." T. Seuss

I believe God gives us the blessing of these little signs as strength in the moment. In hindsight, many signs throughout life prepared me for Lucas, Jason, and even my life as a mom to many children. As a teenager I felt compelled to teach a special needs Sunday school class. I had inscribed on Jason's wedding ring words that many considered morbid: "Till death do us part." And most significantly to the present day, I am the oldest of twelve children. But I'm getting ahead of myself.

The first month, I slept. I recall spending an excessive amount of time in bed after the drain I had felt from the previous three years. I went to bed at 10 p.m., arose with Lucas at 7:30 a.m., put him on the bus at 8 a.m., and crawled back into bed until 9 a.m. when Mabel or Joshua would wake up. Nap time would roll around for the two of them, and I would sink back into bed and sleep until they woke up. The most embarrassing part was that I was so exhausted my seven-year-old would get himself ready for school at 6:30 in the morning and grab a Pop Tart before he walked to the bus stop at the end of the road. What in the world was I thinking? What kind of a mother allows that? I guess one who is so entirely exhausted she is out of options. Caleb never complained; he accepted that I needed to rest.

He and I both felt a sense of relief in those first weeks. He had been called on many times to act older than his seven years, and he was usually my go-to guy with any help I required with Lucas, Mabel, or Joshua. He had also assisted often in getting his father back into bed when he fell, feeding him, or bringing him something if he requested it. We never talked about the relief, but the feeling was there, a guilty relief that it was over.

One evening we took a family walk to the cemetery where Jason was buried, and as Caleb and I sat beside the grave site, I asked, "What do you think?" His response was so appropriate: "It's just dirt, Mom." He was right: it was just dirt. Jason was not there. There was a pile of dirt with a simple headstone, and out of reverence for our traditions surrounding death, we were there paying our respects. But Jason wasn't. The ceremony felt strange, our new life was strange, but Caleb and I knew that life continued.

We stood, took hold of the two strollers holding Josh and Lucas, called out to Mabel, who was running around the lawn, and put one foot in front of the other as we headed home, one step at a time, slowly learning to navigate this new world we were called to embark in.

I would frequently sit in the quiet of the nights, after the kids had gone to bed, after the dim light from the computer screen had faded. I found that I missed Jason—a lot—and that I was lonely, but I did not miss sick Jason. I missed the man I had married, I missed my kids' dad, I missed my friend, but I would not have asked for him back the way he was. My faith absolutely knew that he was completely healed, and my selfishness did not want him back in a cancer-ridden body.

I began to view Jason's healing as a type of salvation. Salvation is completely undeserved and completely grace driven. I did nothing to be deserving of this perfect gift from my Maker; and in fact, I did everything to be undeserving of it! Jason's healing was also like this. Healing, however it comes, is a representation of God's grace. If it is granted on earth, it is an imperfect healing; and in the grand scheme, not the best that God has for his people. If healing comes eternally, it is also connected to grace and salvation, for they who are in Christ Jesus will experience the ultimate healing—body, soul, and spirit—when they enter the throne room of the Redeemer.

In these quiet moments of reflection, this is how I began to accept Jason's death as I renewed my mind to understand that it was not in fact a death at all, but instead it was the rebirth that Jason had often spoken of, and in this rebirth he had received the best healing God could have given.

The kids dealt with it very differently. Caleb had been on the journey with me for the past three years, so he had processed along the way, just as I had. Joshua was not really affected, not having had a strong bond with the stranger who had lain in our office for the past few months. Mabel and Lucas were extremely confused. Three-year-old Mabel and six-year-old Lucas could not figure out where their daddy had gone, and there was no coherent way to explain it to them. Mabel became repetitive in her questions of where and why, and Lucas screamed over the newness of having Mom all the time instead of Dad. I had to overcome the hurdle of reacquainting myself with him after allowing Jason to tend to most of his needs over the past several years. The process was slow going, but he and I reached an understanding shortly after Jason died where he began to accept that he now had Mom, and I would come through for him just as Dad had in the past.

Lucas has become a living, breathing testimony to the glory and power of God. The enemy's authority to kill, steal, or destroy was demolished, maybe not in the way I envisioned, but that is not because of a lack of faith. Faith, I've learned, is standing firm in the knowledge that God's will must and will be done, and that I must embrace his control of the situation regardless of my earthly understanding.

In those first weeks, I beseeched God for wisdom in my life as a single mom. My prayers also included a desperate yearning for strength to be able to walk through whatever I was called to endure—to hear at the end of all I am and all I do those coveted words from my Savior: "Well done, good and faithful servant." This prayer specifically had been evolving within my spirit as the years passed. One day I put words to my thoughts:

> Lord, use me today. Everything within me I give to you for your use and for your glory. Use my life, every single aspect of it. The good, the bad, the ugly, the pains, the deep scars, the beautiful circumstances, my actions, my inactions, my words and thoughts, my obedience, or lack of obedience—may it all be used for your glory and to further your kingdom. Use my past, my present and my future to further ignite the ultimate cause—grace heaped upon grace reaching to the farthest corners of this planet and within the darkest crevices of the human soul. Use the fight in me always for good and never for evil, and use my strength to serve as a battle shield against the fiery darts of the evil one. May I never look at life with purely earthly eyes, but always allow me to see beyond the here and now and to grasp the big picture even if I don't understand it in the moment. Wring my cells, my heart, my mind, my soul, completely empty of everything that can be used, every single drop of talent or ability. It is yours, Lord. May I always give you all the glory until I breathe my last, you call me home, and I leave behind only a pile of nothingness as your heavenly angels escort me to your presence. And last but not least, may I hear the words that every servant of the Most High God yearns to hear one day: "Well done, good and faithful servant." To him be the glory and the honor and the power forever and ever, amen.

CHAPTER 23

Sunlight Burning at Midnight

"He rewards those who earnestly seek him."

Hebrews 11:6

Life continued.

As much as I wished it would stand still and acknowledge my pain and the suffering my children and I had been through—as much as I wished it would acknowledge and pay respect to all of that, life did not. It moved forward, and we all either had to move with it or reside in a self-induced prison created by the deadening of our souls as we raged against the injustice of it all.

The weather cooled, and fall began to make its presence known. I found a new kind of normal, a single mom normal, and a normal where cancer was no longer a part of the daily grind. While I mourned deeply for the loss of my best friend, I also felt that I would not be alone for long. I desperately wanted a lifelong partner and friend to walk beside me once again. Even Jason's mom, Holly, had informed me that she was praying for my future husband because, in her words, "You need a husband and the kids need a dad."

I was tempted to take matters into my own hands one lonely night as I surfed around on a popular dating site, getting an idea of what was available for a widow with four children. Surprisingly, there were quite a few widowers on these sites. I found one attractive man who had been widowed a few months prior, and for an instant I was tempted to start an account.

As I entertained the thought, I heard a stern *No* in my spirit, along with, *If I don't come through by January, you can take matters into your own hands.*

I knew what had just happened: God had spoken to me. Not necessarily in an audible voice, but in the still, small voice that the Bible talks about.

At first I didn't really like it: I wanted to fix the problem of not having a husband, just like I had wanted to fix the problem of having a sick baby or fix my cancer-ridden husband. If I had gone down that road, I probably could have gotten a date with another human being as desperate as myself. Honestly, I just didn't want to be alone anymore! But God had a bigger plan than I could have ever imagined on that lonely evening.

September 29

Five weeks . . . amazing. I don't have days where it feels like yesterday; it always feels like forever ago. The kids and I are managing . . . surprisingly, because I never thought I could do it on my own, but I am doing it. I have about one hundred and fifty volunteers signed up on my website to help out. Thank you to all of you! You have carried me this past year, and I continue to ride upon your shoulders. So yes, we're still doing okay. My master's class gives me something to focus on at night when the house is quiet and I can no longer stuff my feelings away to tend to the chaotic busyness. I can sum up life right now based on two most recent Google searches: first, "best under-eye concealer on the market" and second, "when do most children get all of their teeth in?" In other words, I'm tired. If I could just get the sleep I desperately need I could manage, but man, sleep deprivation is the pits. It's hard enough being a single mom without being so dead tired.

The golf outing fundraiser was a huge success, and now that things are calming down I'm trying to figure out ways to make my life a little easier. I try to get out once a week or I go stir-crazy. I've also hired someone to help with cleaning, which has freed me up tremendously to be able to focus on making memories with the kids and not obsessing about the cleanliness of my house.

Besides that, I think I'm doing okay because I have a lot of life to live yet. Jason was a wonderful chapter, but there are many pages to turn in this book (God willing), and on his deathbed he gave me, I believe, a glimpse of some of those pages. That is a gift that I will forever treasure. He knew I needed that, my personality needed to know it would be okay, and he also knew that my faith would accept it. I'm young; I could potentially have two great loves in my life and could possibly celebrate a fifty-year wedding anniversary with someone. How wonderful would that be? It would be a huge blessing that I'm praying and hoping for. I loved being married; I had a good marriage, which makes marriage very appealing to me again. If I had been in an abusive situation I wouldn't crave it again, but I wasn't. Jason was a testament to marriage; he was a fantastic husband and a great father. Caleb wants a dad again, another testament to what a great dad Jason was. He likes the idea of having a dad, because his experience with a father was a good one. Yes, God is a husband to the widow (a word I detest!) and a father to the fatherless but . . . if I'm honest, it's not quite the same thing. God gives a peace about the situation, but it's a different sort of companionship. God made Adam a helpmate because he knew that we as humans would benefit and get enjoyment from that.

So yes, I'd like another helpmate at some point. I enjoyed marriage, I enjoyed knowing that there was someone I could trust completely and raise my children with, and I would be blessed to experience a good marriage again in my life.

I don't know why I had to go through two very different, yet similar, situations regarding healing in my short stint here so far—one with my son's brain issues and one with my husband's, both bringing about very different results. With Lucas we were told he would never be born because of the severe cerebrospinal buildup in his brain, and he came home from the hospital on August 30, 2004, after eighteen days in neonatal. He was my miracle baby, touched by the Healer. Jason Crisman, his father, after being told that the average life expectancy for his type of brain cancer was fifteen months, went home on August 24, 2010, when he was also touched by the Ultimate Healer. Most would say that Lucas was the answered prayer. I tend to think that Christ and Jason get a good laugh out of this foolish assumption on our part. I don't know if I'm supposed to do something with these experiences, all I know is that it's all a small piece of the never-ending story. It's a very big picture that I'm grasping a little better as I get older, but just a little.

My big procrastination project right now has been working on Jason's headstone. I don't want to use the word *died* on it because I don't believe in that word, so I decided not to. Instead I'm putting "Born on June 2, 1977, and reborn into eternity on August 24, 2010." Those terms (*dead* and *died*) are strange, because I know that he is more alive than any of us. I think we have it backwards. When a baby is born into this life it would make more sense to say, "A baby died into this life of hardship, pain, and suffering," and when someone passes from this life to eternity they enter everlasting, sinless, pain-free life. That's true life. This life is just a glimpse in the grand scheme.

In one sense it's freeing to live like that, but in another I'm having a harder time finding joy. There's such an empty ache right now because he's not here. At times I sense his presence, but I go back and forth with the whole idea that he visits us.

I know I overanalyze everything and should probably just stop thinking so much, but a movie like *Ghost* takes on a whole new meaning when you've lost a loved one. I don't believe in the concept of ghosts, but can his spirit come back to us? Watch over us? See his children grow? Make sure we're okay? I've always said no before he left; now I sense his presence at certain times. Maybe it's just an overactive imagination, I don't know. Maybe death is just a really thin veil between the worlds, and he won't actually miss out on anything, he'll see it all from the grandstands. Maybe. It's a nice thought at times, and then there are other times when I think it would be nice if he didn't have this ability, because it puts me on my best behavior thinking that he could possibly be watching me all the time! It's funny to think of him as having superpowers, because he always said he was Superman.

The kids and I sat down to dinner one Sunday night, and Caleb pulled out a chair for Dad because I made Jason's favorite meal. We all joked around, talking to Dad, asking him about heaven, and Caleb even went up to him and started wrestling with the air. And then Caleb and I were both astonished when Lucas looked straight at the chair for a good five minutes, just intently looking at it, like there was something or someone there. Caleb said, "I think he sees Dad," and then said, "I wish God would give me a vision." I didn't even know that he knew what a vision was! Needless to say, I think his dad could have been there enjoying fettuccine alfredo, and the miraculous part of the whole night was that every child cleaned their entire plate, even Mabel, who never eats anything!

If I'm honest, though, I have a hard time believing that he comes back. I do believe that his spirit will linger in our home for a while, like a scented candle that's blown out. The sweet smell lingers, but the fact remains, the candle's flame has been snuffed out. I don't see how he could visit when the Bible says that there will be no tears or sorrow in heaven. If he saw his daughter, curled up on the couch in depression saying over and over, "I miss my daddy," that would make him sad. If he saw me during a bad moment saying under my breath, "This single parenting thing sucks," that would break his heart, or if he saw his oldest son acting out because he doesn't have a male figure to put him in line anymore, he would be angry.

So no, I think what he had here will linger for a while, which is comforting, but I don't think his presence will stay forever. And maybe it's best that way, for how else could we eventually move on? I've lived through a life already that would make many elderly people cringe, and I'm still standing and breathing and living, and that's what makes me so fearless now. I've been to hell and back in this space-time continuum, to quote Jason. And since I've knelt beside death and literally looked it in the face, and damned it back to where it came from, there's not much left to fear in my remaining years, and that's extremely liberating as a thirty-three-year old. All the ridiculous stuff we think is worth our stress is seriously laughable. All that matters at the end is how we've loved God, how we've loved others, and how we've sought to serve others humbly through our short existence. That's my two cents for today. Just keep livin'!

I ended this particular journal entry with what became my motto during those days and is still my heartfelt mantra to this day: "Just keep livin'!" It's a simple twist on the movie *Finding Nemo*, which I watched with my children one particularly difficult day while their father was battling brain cancer. The loveable character Dorie admonishes the young Nemo during a trying time to "Just keep swimming, swimming, swimming," and I thought to myself, "Just keep living, living, living . . ." I would remind myself of this mantra often, and it became an encouraging admonishment as I walked through some dark valleys.

* * *

On October 31, 2010, I took the kids out for a night of trick or treating. We all pretended like everything was great. I plastered a big, fake smile on my face and took lots of pictures to post on Facebook so that everyone in my social media circle would know I was doing fine, so fine that I had successfully managed to costume four restless little people and embark on a rainy Halloween night to acquire gobs of sweetened morsels that would only entice me worse than the kids in the coming days and weeks.

The kids and I enjoyed the crisp air that November brought, and we spent many of these evenings walking to the cemetery before retiring with warm baths, good-night hugs, and sweet kisses.

One night, November 2 to be exact, I sat down at the computer and was surprised to see an interesting message on the Carepages blog I had kept—a message from a woman who lived in Pennsylvania. She had followed my ramblings and often left encouraging messages, lifting me up in prayer and checking in. I usually didn't have time to read all of the messages, there were so many, but on this particular night I did, and I didn't want to watch television. I rarely watched television . . . the simple act reminded me of how alone I was. I preferred to be on the computer interacting with Facebook friends, instant messaging, or emailing people. At least I felt as if I was with another human being through these outlets.

I stared at the message in front of me, and something about it stirred in my heart. It said:

> You don't know me so, I have no right to do this except I just feel compelled to ask you to go to a website called *The Ronnes*. He is a young widower going through what you are/have and is struggling, and I just thought you might be in a unique position to offer some help. You are an amazingly strong woman, a complete inspiration to me and I wish you all the best. Praying for your continued strength.

That was the start of God revealing to me, in a real way, his faithfulness to those who put their trust in him. It was also the beginning of an amazing love affair with a complete stranger from Oklahoma that would surpass all of my wildest dreams and expectations.

Ryan Ronne, a widower with three small children, had lost his wife to brain cancer four days after Jason died. He and I had shared similar cancer paths from April to the end of August, and we both found blogging to be a therapeutic avenue in which to work through our grief. The initial note from that stranger in Pennsylvania led to me leaving a note of encouragement on his blog, which led to emails, phone calls, and a nerve-wracking meeting in Savannah, Georgia, where we contemplated getting married on our first official date.

Ours was a whirlwind courtship full of friendship, love, romance, passion, tears, sorrow, and joy. We traveled back and forth to one another throughout the following weeks. The initial meeting with the children occurred in late December, when Ryan flew to Michigan and met my kids for the first time, including Lucas, whom I was incredibly nervous about. I wondered what Ryan would think of my miracle child.

When the two met, Lucas was exceptionally obnoxious and screamed about everything. I was an emotional wreck and knew Lucas's attitude had to be a deal breaker. I thought, *What guy in his right mind would want to deal with a kid like this for the rest of his life?* I kept reassuring Ryan that Lucas did not normally act this way and that something had to be wrong—which I found out later was an accurate statement, with yet another ear infection diagnosis. But Ryan didn't shy away.

Other than that first time, Lucas took to Ryan immediately, even allowing him to tuck him into bed the first night and yelling out "Daddy, Daddy" as he walked away. Ryan never flinched at the thought of having to take care of a severely handicapped child. He dove right in as if Lucas were any other child. He asked questions when he was unsure, and to this day, he has done everything in his power to connect with my special boy while trying to understand his needs.

Ryan is a significant part of God displaying his faithfulness to me. He was the answer to Holly's prayer: A godly man, a man immediately invested in my children as much as he was invested in me, a faithful man who could intimately understand my pain because he had recently walked the same road, the ultimate gift from my heavenly Father to me—not just someone to fill the role of husband and Dad but a man I truly, deeply loved and wanted to spend the rest of my life with. I—we—wanted to make our two stories of pain and heartache into something beautiful, something authentic, and something as stunning as sunlight burning at midnight.

CHAPTER 24

A New Beginning

"Jesus said, 'Everything is possible for him who believes.'"

Mark 9:23

Everything I have been through has brought me to this point in life, and he who began a good work in me will be faithful to complete it (Philippians 1:6). I do not live in the painful moments of the past, I don't dwell in the agony of my fearful pregnancy, and I do not live in the defeat of Jason's death. I do not allow those horrific moments to define me.

Each of those terrible events is a piece of the puzzle, but they certainly do not make up the whole of who I am in the present. I honor the past; I acknowledge it; but I will not wallow in it, trying to make myself sad over what has been lost. Life is not always fair, but God's will is always supreme.

As the great king declares in Ecclesiastes 3:4, there is "a time to mourn and a time to dance." I am now dancing.

* * *

Ryan and I were engaged in January of 2011. We married on April 22 of the same year and started our fairy-tale life together, living happily ever after. Oh wait, that's not exactly how it went. We had our issues. Many issues, including grief, blending families, childhood demons, twenty grandparents, seven grieving kids, and the list could go on and on . . . but everything has been worth the price.

On August 14, 2012, two days after his eighth birthday, Lucas was legally adopted by his new dad Ryan, along with the rest of the gang, and the baton was officially passed from one man to the next. I also had the privilege of adopting Ryan's three biological children, Tate, Mya, and Jada, who I am honored to be a mom to in this next leg of our journey as a family. The same summer, all eight of us cheered Lucas on as he walked approximately fifty feet across our driveway completely unassisted, a symbol of hope against all odds.

While Ryan and I get to experience the joy of walking with Lucas on earth, there is another person I am convinced is eagerly awaiting his chance to walk with him as well. Without a doubt, Jason and Lucas will walk hand in hand down the streets of gold—but not too soon. Lucas has a lot of living to do yet, as do I, a new wife and mom of seven.

But that's another story for another day.

EPILOGUE

Beauty from Ashes

"And provide for those who grieve in Zion—
to bestow on them a crown of beauty
instead of ashes,
the oil of joy
instead of mourning,
and a garment of praise
instead of a spirit of despair."

Isaiah 61:3

I have now been a mother to a severely handicapped child for the past twelve years. Not an easy task, but it's not hard either. It's a constant contradiction in terms.

As a parent to a handicapped child, I've become incredibly thankful for the small, seemingly insignificant accomplishments that Lucas has achieved, such as saying a few words, holding his head up, sitting without falling, and eventually being able to walk . . . at eight years old.

Lucas lives in Lucas's own world. He doesn't feel deprived of what he doesn't know, and he has absolutely no pretensions or ulterior motives toward anything or anyone. He is what he is; happy with VeggieTales, food, a clean diaper, and chocolate milk. He has taught me so much about our human ideas of perfection and the standards people have for each other, because Lucas is exactly how God intended him to be. He has touched many lives through his perceived imperfections, and through his life he is a beautiful testimony of God's faithfulness.

Many have questioned the purpose of Lucas's life or quoted the verse "Who sinned, this man or his parents that he was born blind?" (John 9:2), and the answer is exactly as Christ proclaims: "This happened so the work of God might be displayed in his life" (John 9:3). He has not been healed to the extent that I allowed my limited imagination to envision during the pregnancy, but in his years, he has healed me and many others of misconceptions we hold regarding healing and our God.

We have such a limited understanding of the words *healing* and *healed*. Lucas is perfect the way God created him, and every time he surpasses any limitation, his very existence screams glory to God. I don't know what the future looks like for him, but to me he is healed, just as Jason is healed, and just as my life has been healed, like sunlight burning at midnight, a beautifully miraculous experience.

I am going to end with a story I once heard about what it's like to have and raise a special-needs child. This story specifically relates to being a parent of a handicapped child, but I believe its words can be applied to many unique situations that would cause us to question our faith and God's plan for our lives.

Your entire life, you dream of going to Paris, France, and finally save enough money for this vacation. The ticket is bought, the activities planned, and the best hotels and places to eat mapped out. Finally the day arrives. You check in, board the plane, sit for hours, and then finally land, but there has been a huge mistake! Instead of landing in Paris, you land in Rome!

What do you do? You planned for Paris, Paris is your dream, and Paris is where you had your heart set on going. You don't know anything about Rome or what to do in Rome, or where to stay or what to eat in Rome, but you decide to, in spite of your disappointment, make the best of a bad situation and begin your vacation in Rome. You realize after a few days that Rome is not Paris, but Rome has a beauty of its own: sights, sounds, and traditions making it lovely and magical, a spectacular vacation in its own right.

I believe it's the same with the special children God gives us or the twists and turns he allows in our lives. At first, the news brings devastation because it's not Paris, it's not the "normal," healthy child everyone wants or the "normal," traditional family everyone else seems to have, or whatever "normal" we may be coveting. It is different than what we plan for in our lives, but ultimately we have to embrace the fact that Rome and these children and our circumstances can be just as beautiful and fulfilling as Paris, and perhaps, just perhaps, even better than Paris ever would have been for us.

This isn't to say that I don't still have moments where I wrestle with God's will or have difficulty trusting his plan. He has blessed me richly, turned my mourning into gladness and my ashes into something beautiful, yet I do have moments of fear as I wonder, *What will he require of me next?* It is a faith journey that I am continuously walking through, step by step, as my faith grows and matures through the years and the experiences.

May we each walk hand in hand with our Savior every day, trusting his will for our lives, in Paris or in Rome or in whatever city he may call us to explore, remembering to enjoy the journey, relish the adventure, and never back down from the overflowing blessings God has in store for our lives. Never, ever lose hope. Thank you, Lord, for restoring what the locust had eaten.

I still ask to see angels all the time, but I have yet to see one. Many days I look up to the heavens, and I can feel a thin, translucent barrier separating it all, the earth from the heavens above, and I know there are multitudes of angels staring back. I beg and plead, "Please Lord, let me see one," but I have not, not yet at least. I believe some of the same angels who watched over Lucas during those first fragile moments also comforted his birth father years later as he wrestled with his final moments in our fallen world. I believe many of them ultimately lifted his spirit from his decaying, sick, cancer-ridden body and escorted him to his eternal reward. I have never felt so alive and raw as I did in those moments of watching what life is truly about through Jason—running our races and receiving the crown from the One we serve.

I am honored and humbled that I was able to help escort Jason into his eternal reward. God's power was perfected in my weakness. He stripped me of everything I thought could remedy the problem. He stripped me of all I held dear in this life—a perfect family and healthy children. He stripped me of control, worry, and the need to fix every problem with formulas and all of the latest and greatest research. He stripped me of a prideful attitude and arrogant thinking that reasoned I could actually do something to fix the problem. He stripped me until I was down to absolutely nothing, spiritually and emotionally vulnerable, and all I had left was him.

At that point I discovered he was all I had ever needed.

Finally, may you remember these words:

Just keep livin'!

Jess can be found sharing her adventures at:
www.jessplusthemess.com
She also spends way too much time on social media sites:
Facebook.com/jessplusthemess
Twitter.com/jessplusthemess
Instagram.com/jessplusthemess
She will occasionally remember to check her email inquiries at:
jessplusthemess@gmail.com

Lucas is born.

First official family picture.   I'm
about 8 weeks pregnant with Mabel
here. (Photo: Randy Johnson)

Lucas after his chiari malformation and tethered spinal cord surgery. Caleb entertaining him.

A few months before the brain tumor is discovered. Jason was starting to rapidly lose weight and suffer from headaches.

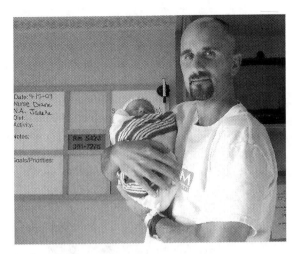

Joshua is born.

First complete family picture after surgery and Joshua's birth. (Photo: Jen Konyndyk)

My all-time favorite photo of Jason with his princess. (Photo: Jen Konyndyk)

Note
Dear, dad I

hope you feal
better soon. It
feals like your
toomer is get
ing worse, I.v. had
a fun time whith
you. Thanks for
evrything youve
given me. well
get well.

Letter Caleb wrote Jason during the summer of 2010 as the end was drawing near.

Our last family picture. (Photo: Jen Konyndyk)

Caleb at his dad's funeral, preparing to throw a yellow
rose into the ground. (Photo: Ewelina Konyndyk)

Me comforting Mabel at her daddy's funeral. (Photo: Ewelina Konyndyk)

My first Halloween as a widow. This was the night I searched for the Ronne blog after getting the kids to bed.

The first time I met Ryan, in Savannah, Georgia.

First time I flew Caleb and Mabel to Oklahoma to meet Ryan and the kids, January 2011.

In 2015, Ryan and I greeted Annabelle, making us parents of eight. In many ways, our adventures are just beginning!